TableFlowers

TischBlumen

Conception and Floristics
Konzeption und Floristik

Frank Pieper

Die Deutsche Bibliothek - CIP-Einheitsaufnahme

Tischblumen : zeitgemäße Tischdekoration durch die Jahreszeiten = **Tableflowers** / [Fotos Patrick-Pantze-Werbefotografie GmbH, Lage. Gesamtleitung Klaus Wagener. Text Hella Henckel-Bruckhaus. Übers. Janet Brümmer]. - 1. Aufl. - Braunschweig : Thalacker-Medien, 2000
ISBN 3-87815-154-3

Gesamtleitung / Direction
    Klaus Wagener, Floristik Marketing Service GmbH (FMS), Ratingen.

Konzeption+Floristik / Concept+Floristics
    Frank Pieper, Münster.

Text / Text
    Hella Henckel-Bruckhaus, Ratingen.

Grafische Gestaltung / Layout Design
    DART-Werbekonzepte, Krefeld.

Fotos / Photos
    Patrick Pantze Werbefotografie GmbH, Lage.

Druck / Printing
    Print Partner, Bocholt.

Übersetzung / Translation
    Janet Brümmer, BA, Düsseldorf.

© 2000 Floristik Marketing Service GmbH (FMS)
Am Potekamp 6 – D-40885 Ratingen / Germany
Tel.: +49-2102-9644-0, Fax +49-2102-896073
1. Auflage 2000

ISBN 3-87815-154-3

Das Werk ist urheberrechtlich geschützt. Jede Verwertung ist ohne Zustimmung des Verlages oder des Herausgebers unzulässig und strafbar. Das gilt insbesondere für die Vervielfältigung, Übersetzungen, Mikroverfilmungen und die Einspeicherung und Verarbeitung in elektronischen Systemen.

All rights reserved. No part of this publication may be reproduced, stored in a retrieval system, or transmitted, in any form by any means, electronic, mechanical, photocopying, recording or otherwise without the written permission of the publisher.

8-41 FrühlingsErwachen
SpringAwakening

Frühlingsgäste
Spring guests

Herzensangelegenheiten
Affairs of the heart

Allerlei Ei
Eggs'n stuff

Tulpenbuffet
Tulip buffet

Muttertags-Frühstück
Mother's Day breakfast

42-75 SommerGäste
SummerGuests

Sommergarten
Summer garden

Margeritentafel
Marguerite table

Sommerreigen
Summer dance

Solistentreffen
Solo players

Blütenromanze
Floral romance

76-109 HerbstFeste
AutumnFestivities

Klassische Hochzeit
Classic wedding

Formvollendete Verlobung
Engagement party in perfect form

Liebliche Taufe
Sweet and charming baptism.

Farbenprächtiges Jubiläum
Jubilee in resplendent colours

Stimmungsvoller Geburtstag
Birthday party full of atmosphere

110-143 WinterRendezvous
WinterRendezvous

Purpurne Tafelpracht
Table in magnificent purple

Adventstee-Einladung
Invitation to Advent tea

Weihnachts-Rendezvous
Christmas rendezvous

Sternstunde der TischArt
Star-studded table art

Happy New Year
Happy New Year

Enjoying good food in an inviting atmosphere is an important part of life in our culture. The "how and wherefore" is an expression of our lifestyle and our individuality. Many people today feel the need for a meal taken together to be more than just a culinary experience – it must also be a feast for the eyes. Savouring with all the senses, and combining eating, drinking and everything around you into a harmonious whole – that is the art of fine dining.

And flowers are the stars of the show when it comes to sensual and captivating table decorations. Not that these must be full of pomp and splendour. Even a simple garden table that invites you to sit for a while under a shady tree in summer can be transformed into a uniquely beautiful dining table with the help of a few blossoms from your garden, a meadow or alongside a field. This book, conceptualized and designed by stylist and master florist Frank Pieper, illustrates how the most beautiful table decorations can be often created almost effortlessly with a clever new idea. And you needn't be an expert florist to try out these arrangements or use the inspirations for your own creations.

TableFlowers is a book for the many different occasions where people gather at table, whether for an afternoon tea party or dinner in the evening. If you are planning table decorations for a get-together in the intimate circle of your family or a more formal occasion with friends or business partners, this is the ideal book for you.

Chock full of great ideas, it will motivate everyone who picks it up to try their hand at creating table decorations of their own.

Flowers invite the guests to table
Blüten laden zu Tisch

Essen und Genießen sind ein wesentlicher Bestandteil unserer Lebenskultur. Das „Wie" ist Ausdruck unseres Lebensstils und unserer Individualität. Vielen Menschen ist es heute ein großes Bedürfnis, gemeinsames Essen nicht nur kulinarisch zu einem Erlebnis werden zu lassen, sondern auch zu einem Augenschmaus. Mit allen Sinnen genießen, Essen, Trinken und das Drumherum zu einem harmonischen Ganzen zu komponieren, ist die Kunst rund um Tisch und Tafel. Dabei spielen Blumen ihre Paraderolle. Sie sind die Nummer eins, wenn es um sinnliche und verzaubernde Tischdekoration geht. Sie muss nicht unbedingt mit Prunk und Pracht verbunden sein. Selbst ein einfacher Gartentisch, der zu einem sommerlichen Kaffeetrinken im Grünen einlädt, kann mit ein paar Blüten aus dem eigenen Garten, von Wiese oder Feldrain zu einer schönen Tafel werden.

Stylist und Floristmeister Frank Pieper zeigt in diesem Buch, dass es meist nur die pfiffige Idee ist, die mit wenigen Handgriffen verwirklicht, traumhaft schöne und begeisternde Tafeldekorationen entstehen läßt. Man muss auch kein Blumenkünstler sein, um das Gezeigte einmal selbst auszuprobieren oder als Ideenanstoß für eigene Kreationen nehmen zu können.

TischBlumen ist ein Buch für viele Anlässe rund um Tisch und Tafel, egal ob Sie zum traditionellen Kaffeekränzchen oder zum abendlichen Diner laden, ob Sie im kleinen, intimen Familienkreis feiern oder anläßlich einer repräsentativen Einladung im Bekanntenkreis Ihre Tischdekoration planen. Es ist ein Buch, das viele Ideen rund um Blume und Pflanze zeigt und jeden motivieren will, sich mit blumigen Tafelfreuden selbst einmal zu beschäftigen.

SpringAwakening
FrühlingsErwachen

Delicate colours in full force: the symbols of spring. After the dreary, colourless winter, every spot of colour is especially refreshing! But don't think for a moment that springtime has only delicate and light colours on hand. The spectrum of blues and violet tones also represents this awakening and burgeoning season, thanks to the *Hyacinth*, *Muscari*, *Anemone* or crocus – but to name a few. Green in combination with pure white exudes an aura of purity, clarity, vitality and a reawakening of joie de vivre. In this respect, spring has much to choose from, as so many kinds of flowers are also found in white, for example the *Anemone*, freesia, *Hyacinth*, narcissus, snowdrops or daffodils. The most important harbinger of spring is without a doubt the tulip, usually dressed in luminous shades of red, orange or yellow. They enrich the otherwise cool spring atmosphere with their warm tones, spreading warmth and comfort on early spring days when there is still a nip in the air.

Our table decorations illustrate this spring-like diversity of flowers with all their colour variations.

Spring guests, a symphony with fresh blue and delicate green, reflecting the coolness and also the lightness of the first season of the year.
Affairs of the heart, a warm sensual declaration full of the power of the colour spectrum from rosé and pure red to bright orange.
Eggs 'n stuff, the fun and teasing decoration idea that heralds the festive aspects of spring with soft-looking green-and-white and a touch of yellow.
Tulip buffet, drummer absolute among the spring messengers. Striving upwards in their representation, self-confident in their colour composition and simply extraordinary.
Mother's Day breakfast, the ambience of natural white and the charm of the graceful lily of the valley set the mood for this table idea with its natural colours and ambience.

Zarte Farben in voller Macht: Das symbolisiert den Frühling. Nach der trüben, farblosen Winterzeit wirkt jeder Farbtupfer jetzt besonders erfrischend! Doch man sollte nicht meinen, dass der Frühling nur die zarten und leichten Couleurs parat hält. Auch die Palette der Blau- bis Violetttöne repräsentiert die aufbrechende Jahreszeit, man denke nur an Hyazinthe, *Muscari*, Anemone oder auch Krokusse. Grün in Kombination mit reinem Weiß strahlt Reinheit, Klarheit, Vitalität und die wiedererwachende Lebensfreude aus. Hier hat der Frühling viel zu bieten, denn so manche Blume hat auch ihre weißblühenden Vertreter, seien es Anemonen, Freesien, Hyazinthen, Narzissen, Schneeglöckchen oder Märzenbecher. Die wichtigsten Frühlingsboten sind sicherlich die Tulpen, die sich meist in leuchtendes Rot, Orange bis strahlendes Gelb kleiden. Sie bereichern die Palette der eher kalt wirkenden um die der warmen Töne und verbreiten damit Wärme und Wohlbehagen auch in den noch kühlen Frühlingstagen.

Unsere Tischdekorationen zeigen diese frühlingshafte Blütenvielfalt und ihre Farbvarianten auf.

Frühlingsgäste, eine Symphonie mit frischem Blau und zartem Grün, die Kühle und gleichzeitige Helligkeit der ersten Jahreszeit widerspiegelnd.
Herzensangelegenheiten, ein warmes, sinnliches Bekenntnis, das mit der Macht der Farben von zartem Rosé über reines Rot bis zum kräftigen Orange agiert.
Allerlei Ei, die augenzwinkernde Dekorationsidee, die in softig erscheinendem Grünweiß und einem Akzent Gelb von der festlichen Seite des Frühlings kündet.
Tulpenbuffet, ein Paukenschlag der Frühlingsboten schlechthin. Aufwärtsstrebend in der Darstellung, selbstbewußt in der Farbkomposition und einfach ungewöhnlich.
Muttertags-Frühstück, die Anmut des naturreinen Weiß' und der Liebreiz des Maiglöckchens bestimmen eine in Farbe und Ausstrahlung sehr natürlich gehaltene Tischidee.

Affairs of the heart
Herzensang

Spring guests
Frühlingsgäste

SpringAwakening
FrühlingsErwachen

Tulip buffet
Tulpenbuffet

genheiten

Eggs'n stuff
Allerlei Ei

Mother`s Day breakfast
Muttertags-Frühstück

square glass containers (Kayak), KPM `Berlin` dishes (Becker), Wilkens cutlery (Becker)

*Glasquader (Kayak), Geschirr KPM `Berlin`
(Becker), Besteck Wilkens (Becker)*

Spring guests

Frühlingsgäste

Guests in spring. For special friends you want everything to run smoothly. Light and brightness on the table, with clear and well-matched decorations. This best suits the new awakenings of nature going on outside the door. And what else could symbolize such burgeoning energy better than these first spring flowers complete with bulbs? Freed from all clinging earth and arranged in square glass vases full of water, they provide a decorative highlight for the tone-in-tone colours of the *Anemone*, forget-me-nots and freesia blossoms. Particularly the luminous blue associates the freshness of awakening spring in a special way.

Frühlingsgäste! Da soll es in jeder Hinsicht unkompliziert zugehen. Licht und hell auf dem Tisch, klar und gegliedert in der Dekoration selbst. Das paßt am besten zum Aufbruch, der sich jetzt in der Natur draußen vollzieht.
Und was könnte die sprießende Energie besser symbolisieren als die ersten Frühjahrsblüher mit ihren Zwiebeln. Von der Erde befreit und in Wasser gefüllte Glasgefäße gestellt sind sie hier zu der Ton-in-Ton-Farbigkeit der Blüten von *Anemone*, Vergissmeinnicht und Freesie der dekorative Hingucker. Vor allem das leuchtende Blau. Das assoziert die Frische des anbrechenden Frühlings in besonderer Weise.

Spring guests. That which normally remains hidden from sight beneath the earth is given a special reception here. The rinsed and sprouting bulbs of hyacinths and *Anaphalis margaritacea* are literally held aloft by the tall table stands. With the name cards displayed on their cone-shaped tips, they serve as stylish "usherettes" for the guests. An unusual and interesting table decoration that is much simpler to create than it appears.

A square metal plate forms the basis of these name card holders. Onto the plate is welded a thin metal pole. Around the upper end is wound a cone of *Tillandsia* and silver wires tapering in towards the bottom. The crowning glory is a dried *Calendula* flower with a flowering *Muscari* bulb on top. No need to worry though: even without an additional water supply, the bulb contains sufficient nutrient reserves to keep the flower fresh for several days.

For the serviette ring, tiny pearl onions are strung on a wire, which is then bent into the shape of a ring and placed around the rolled serviette. A single *Muscari* flower with its bulb cleansed of earth provides the subtle floral accent.

Frühlingsgäste. Das, was sonst in der Erde den Blicken verborgen bleibt, erfährt eine besondere Herausstellung. Die ausgewaschenen und ausgetriebenen Zwiebeln von Hyazinthen und Perlblumen werden mit Hilfe der Tischständer buchstäblich erhöht. An ihren tütenförmigen Enden werden die Namensschilder der Gäste angebracht, so dass sie als stilvolle Platzanweiser dienen. Eine ungewöhnliche wie interessante Tischdekoration, die viel einfacher zu erstellen ist als sie aussieht.

Eine quadratische Metallplatte bildet die Basis der Namensschildständer. Hierauf ist ein Metallstab geschweißt. Sein oberes Ende wird mit *Tillandsia* und Silberdraht, sich nach oben hin verbreiternd, umwickelt. Den Abschluß bildet eine aufgeklebte, getrocknete *Calendula*-Blüte, auf die die ausgetriebene *Muscari*-Zwiebel gesteckt ist. Keine Sorge, die Zwiebel enthält ausreichend Nährstoffreserven, um die Blüte auch ohne Wasserzufuhr über mehrere Tage hinweg frisch zu erhalten. Für den Serviettenring werden kleine Perlzwiebeln auf einen Draht gesteckt, dieser zum Ring gebogen und um die Serviettenrolle gelegt. Ein einzelner *Muscari*-Stängel mit seiner von Erde befreiten Zwiebel bildet den dezenten Blütenschmuck.

Glasquader, Unterteller (Kayak), Glashaube (Veip), Gläser, graue Teller, Teller mit Silberrand (Haymann), Geschirr KPM `Berlin` (Becker)

square glass containers, saucers (Kayak), glass domes (Veip), glasses, grey plates, plates with silver trim (Haymann), KPM `Berlin` dishes (Becker)

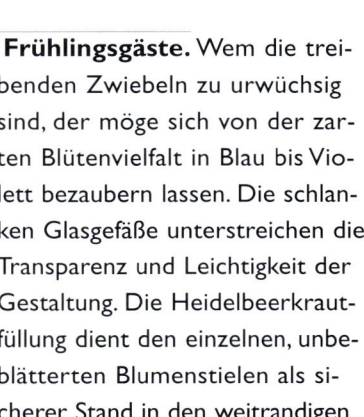

Frühlingsgäste. Wem die treibenden Zwiebeln zu urwüchsig sind, der möge sich von der zarten Blütenvielfalt in Blau bis Violett bezaubern lassen. Die schlanken Glasgefäße unterstreichen die Transparenz und Leichtigkeit der Gestaltung. Die Heidelbeerkrautfüllung dient den einzelnen, unbeblätterten Blumenstielen als sicherer Stand in den weitrandigen Gefäßen.

Ein Bündchen Vergissmeinnicht schmückt die zur Tüte geformte Serviette. Unsichtbar darin verborgen sorgt ein wassergefülltes "Orchideenröhrchen" dafür, dass die zarten Frühlingsblumen länger frisch bleiben.

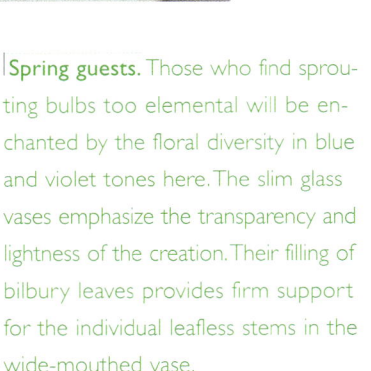

Spring guests. Those who find sprouting bulbs too elemental will be enchanted by the floral diversity in blue and violet tones here. The slim glass vases emphasize the transparency and lightness of the creation. Their filling of bilbury leaves provides firm support for the individual leafless stems in the wide-mouthed vase.

A bunch of forget-me-nots peeks out from inside the serviette rolled into a cone shape. Concealed inside the napkin is a small glass tube filled with water to keep the delicate spring blossoms looking fresh for a long time.

Teller, Leuchter (Des Pots), Kerzen (AV), Rosengefäß (Kayak), Gläser, rote Glasteller (Becker)

plates, candleholders (Des Pots), candles (AV), glass vase (Kayak), glasses, red glass plates (Becker)

Affairs of the heart

Herzensangelegenheiten

Ein überaus herzlicher Empfang, der hier den Tischgästen geboten wird. Dass jeder einzelne von Herzen willkommen ist, machen die Blütenherzen am jeweiligen Platz deutlich. Wie individuell gestaltete Tischkarten wirken die jeder Person bewußt zugedachten Farben. Rot für denjenigen, dem die ganz besondere Aufmerksamkeit gilt – vielleicht dem Herzallerliebsten. Orange für den Gast, der für seine ausgelassene und heitere Lebensart bekannt ist.
Rosé für die Zartbesaitete und Pink für die Spritzige, Quirlige. Bei so viel herzlicher Verbundenheit gehört auch ein warmes Kerzenlicht dazu. Fröhlich und unkompliziert die spielerisch angebrachten Herz-Anhänger an der Tischdecke. Und Rosen dürfen bei so viel Liebelei natürlich keineswegs fehlen.

An extremely hearty reception is extended to the company at table. That everyone here is heartily welcome is made clear by the floral hearts at every place setting. The colours, specially selected for each guest, are like individually-designed name cards. Red for someone close to the heart – perhaps a sweetheart. Orange for the guest known for his exuberance and light-hearted nature. Rosé for a person of sensibility and pink for someone lively and witty. The warm glow of candles provides the right ambience for so much heartfelt affection. Jolly and uncomplicated are the playfully added heart-shaped pendants on the tablecloth. And roses are a must to complete the loving atmosphere.

Herzensangelegenheiten. Maßliebchen, Ranunkeln, Strauchrosen – Blumen, die in ihrer rundlichen, gefüllten Blütenform geradezu naiv und unschuldig wirken und so manches Herz anrühren. Ihr kompakter, markanter Solo-Auftritt duldet keinen weiteren Blütenschmuck auf der Tafel. Deshalb zieren nur noch vereinzelte Rosenblütenblätter das helle Tischtuch. Und getrocknete *Calendula*-Blüten schmücken mit ihrer leuchtenden Farbe die Serviettenspange. Sie ist ganz einfach anzufertigen, indem ein mit Klebstoff bestrichener Holzring mit den Trockenblüten berieselt wird.

Affairs of the heart. Daisies, buttercups, and *Crataegus* roses – flowers which appear almost naïve and innocent with their soft rounded shapes, and touch many a heart. Their compact and striking solo performance will not share the stage with other floral decorations. Therefore only a few single rose petals are strewn on the pale-coloured tablecloth. And dried *Calendula* blossoms decorate the serviette holders with their luminous colours. These are quite simple to make, by smearing a wooden ring with glue and sprinkling it with the dried flowers.

Herzensangelegenheiten. Nahezu unendlich interpretierbar ist das Herzthema für den Tischschmuck. Auch hier wirken das Licht, die Farbe und die Formensprache stimmungsgebend. Die einheitliche Rosengarnierung der verschieden großen und unterschiedlich gefertigten Herzvasen gibt der lebhaften Gestaltung eine Beruhigung. Diese sind aus Kräutern und Sisal mit Hilfe von Silberdraht erstellt. Spiralig geformte „Füßchen" unterstreichen nicht nur die Leichtigkeit, sie bringen auch den augenzwinkernden Witz in die herzige Tischgestaltung. Die prächtige Samtschleife zu der Rose, die in ihrem tütenähnlich umwickelten Glasröhrchen den Serviettenschmuck bildet, untermalt die sinnliche Tischdekoration.

Affairs of the heart. The heart motif for table decorations can be interpreted almost endlessly. Here again the light, colours and shapes set the mood. The uniformity of the heart-shaped vases of various sizes lends a calm note to the otherwise lively creation. These are made of herbs and natural fibres wound about with silver wires. Their spiral-shaped "feet" not only emphasize the lightness, they also add a touch of cheeky wit to this hearty table creation. The luxurious velvet ribbon for the rose, adorning the serviette in its glass tube nestled inside a grassy cone, underscores the sensual table decoration.

candleholders (Des Pots), dishes (Becker), candles (AV)

Leuchter (Des Pots), Geschirr (Becker), Kerzen (AV)

Vase, Teelichter (Kehrle), Geschirr KPM `Berlin` (Becker), Nylonsäckchen (Kayak), Straußen-, Wachteleier (Pinaruh), Stühle (Moulin Galland), Deckelgläser (Veip), Servietten (Henry Dean), Bänder (ABA)

vase, tea candles (Kehrle), KPM `Berlin` dishes (Becker), nylon pot covers (Kayak), ostrich and quail eggs (Pinaruh), chairs (Moulin Galland), covered glasses (Veip), serviettes (Henry Dean), ribbons (ABA)

Eggs 'n stuff

Allerlei Ei

The actors on centre stage here are the egg and the marguerite daisy. Quick and easy to put together, this table decoration is a fresh breeze either for the table in the kitchen or a tastefully appointed living room. And the trick is simply the unconventional combination of the individual components. The delicate lime green, complemented with gentle pastel shades of white, is the colour script. Marguerite, the charming leading lady, fits in well with this light-hearted spring feeling. Freshly picked from a spring meadow, she assumes her place of honour in the egg-shaped vases. A table arrangement reminiscent of Easter that will captivate guests of all ages.

Hier stehen das Ei und die Margerite ganz im Mittelpunkt. Mit wenig Aufwand ist eine Tischdekoration geschaffen, die in der Küche oder selbst im gediegenen Wohnraum Abwechslung auf den Tisch bringt. Und dabei kommt es nur auf das unkonventionelle Zusammenfügen der einzelnen Bestandteile an. Das zarte Limonengrün, pastellig angehaucht mit sanften Weißtönen, ist dabei die farbliche Klammer. In diese frühlingshafte Leichtigkeit paßt sich die liebliche Margerite hervorragend ein. Frisch gepflückt von der Frühlingswiese nimmt sie als Einzeldarstellerin in den Eiervasen geradezu eine bedeutungsvolle Position ein. Nicht nur bei den „Großen", vor allem bei den kleinen Kindern wird solch ein österlich anmutendes Tischarrangement auf Begeisterung stoßen.

Allerlei Ei. Ein Gänseei bildet den Serviettenring, dessen Löcher vergrößert sind. Ein Silbervogel scheint die Feder auf dem *Tillandsia*-Kränzchen zurückgelassen zu haben. Wer nicht über einen solchen verfügt, akzentuiert den Federkiel mit etwas Blattsilber. Wie eine Wiese, auf der diese Straußenei-Vasen für die Margeriten ruhen, wirkt die *Sagina*-Pflanze in den Bechern. Eine schöne Entsprechung zu den gefüllten Nylonsäckchen, die mit einem blattversilberten Ei und dem Namensschild versehen als Gastgeschenk eine bleibende Erinnerung sind. Und wer von der Eierei noch nicht genug hat, versteckt Blumiges in dem großen Drahtei.

Eggs 'n stuff. A goose egg forms the basis for the serviette ring with enlarged openings at either end. A silvery bird appears to have lost a feather on the *Tillandsia* wreath. If such a plume is not readily available, a large feather can be covered with silver leaf.

The *Sagina* plants in the silver cups are like a meadow on which the ostrich-egg vases for the marguerite daisies rest. A lovely accompaniment to the nylon bags, each cradling an egg overlaid with silver leaf with a name card suspended on a green cord, which are original keepsakes for the guests. And those who need more "egging on" will find more flowers and Easter goodies hiding in the oversized wire mesh egg.

Allerlei Ei. Wer es etwas verspielter und lustiger mag, übersteigert die Idee, ausgeblasene Eier zu kleinen Väschen zu machen. Damit diese ihren festen und sicheren Stand bekommen, werden sie in den gläsernen Henkelkorb gestellt. Zusätzlich dekorieren kleine, versilberte oder weiß gestrichene Tontöpfe den Tisch. Einige Tage zuvor wurde Grassamen hinein gestreut, der bei Zimmertemperatur und gut feucht gehalten in wenigen Tagen bereits den frischgrünen Rasenflaum bildet. Noch schneller lassen sich die Töpfe mit Kressesamen begrünen. Aber auch andere Getreidesaaten wie Weizen, Hafer zeigen schnell ihre ersten grünen Spitzen, die unbedingt zu dieser Tischdekoration gehören. Je mehr von dieser einzelnen Dekorationen den Tisch zieren, desto fröhlicher sieht es aus.

Glasdeckel-Kästen (Ikea), Geschirr (Becker), Stühle (Moulin Galland)

Eggs `n stuff. Those who like things a little more playful and fun will love this idea: hollowed eggshells become tiny vases. To prevent them from rolling away they are placed in the glass basket. Small clay pots, overlaid with silver or painted white, additionally decorate the table. A few days before some grass seeds were sown in the pots and now, kept moist at room temperature, they have become fresh green mini-lawns. Garden cress seeds will grow even faster. But other kinds of grains, such as wheat or oats, also show their green sprouts in no time at all, and should definitely be a part of this fun and lively table party. The motto of this table decoration: the more the merrier!

glass basket (Ikea), dishes (Becker), chairs (Moulin Galland)

Particularly when guests are invited for champagne, the buffet should have an impressive effect. On such light-hearted occasions – especially in spring – heavy decorations are not suitable. They must be light and playful. Slim, long-stemmed tulips compete with the tall champagne glasses, stretching their long floral necks upwards. It makes a lovely combination when they are placed singly in the glasses, dressed in bright paper collars to heighten the colour effect. And nothing needs to be arranged in straight rows here. Like guests who mill about the table, the tulips lean towards each other, left and right and centre, as if in conversation. A graceful interplay of flowers, but one which should be carefully watched, as these "guests" can also become tipsy!

glasses (Becker, Pizarro), metal tray (Kehrle), velvet ribbon (Senn), aluminium plate (Des Pots)

Tulip buffet
Tulpenbuffet

Besonders, wenn zu einem Sektempfang geladen wird, sollte die Wirkung des Buffets beeindrucken. Im Frühling und zu einem fröhlich-beschwingten Anlaß passen keine schweren Dekorationen. Da muss es leicht und spielerisch zugehen. Schlanke, stielige Tulpen bieten sich geradezu an, um im Wettstreit mit den langen Sektflöten ihre Blütenhälse in die Höhe zu recken. Ein schönes Miteinander ist es, wenn sie in einzelne Gläser eingestellt werden und ihr Stängel zudem noch in einer bunten Papiertüte steckt. Das steigert die zarte Farbwirkung. Dabei muss nichts in Reih und Glied stehen. So wie die Gäste zufällig miteinander plaudernd sich um das Buffet gruppieren, sind hier Tulpen arrangiert, die eine neigt sich zu ihrer linken, die andere zu ihrer rechten, die dritte nach vorn. Ein graziöses Spiel der Blumen, dem allerdings auch mit Vorsicht wegen der Schwipps- und Umkippgefahr begegnet werden muss.

Gläser (Becker, Pizarro), Zinktablett (Kehrle), Samtband (Senn), Aluminiumteller (Des Pots)

Tulip buffet. Tulips in shades of flaming yellow, fiery red and rosé-violet. The orange and pink shades of the tulips are specially selected to represent a luminous display of fireworks. This daring and altogether unusual colour combination is an absolute eye-catcher. Accessories like the paper cones and the serviette decorations heighten these colourful vibrations even further. The serviette on the tiny wreath of forget-me-nots bears a thick velvet bow in rich violet. The soft warm texture of the cloth is a sensual contrast to the smooth petals of the waxed tulips. An unusual accent which underscores the fresh spring feeling is provided by the decorative dishes full of greenish-white *Viburnum* blossoms. They form the sweet-scented bed for the coloured sceptres, made of scale-like layers of tulip petals and ribbons. A floral jewel for each of the guests, which they can take home with them as a fragrant souvenir of the party.

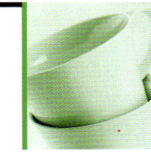

Tulpenbuffet. Gelblich-geflammt, knallrot, bis rosé-violett sind die Tulpenfarben. Bewusst sind für diese Tulpendekoration orange und pinkfarbene ausgesucht worden, die zusammen ein Feuerwerk an Leuchtkraft darstellen. Von dieser gewagten und durchaus unüblichen Farbkombination wird das Auge geradezu angezogen. Accessoires, wie die umhüllenden Tüten und der Serviettenschmuck steigert dieses farbliche Vibrieren. Die Serviette auf dem Blütenring aus Vergissmeinnicht trägt eine dicke violette Samtschleife, die mit ihrer Stofflichkeit dem Wächsernen der Tulpenblütenblätter ein sinnliches Pendant entgegensetzt. Ein ungewöhnlicher Akzent, der aber die frische Frühlingsanmutung unterstützt, sind die mit den weißlichgrünen *Viburnum*-Blüten gefüllten Schmucktellerchen. Sie sind das Bett für die Farbspieße, die aus schuppenartig umlegten Tulpenblütenblättern und Bändern gefertigt wurden. Ein florales Schmuckteil in der Anzahl der Gäste, das von diesen als kleine Erinnerung an die Feier mit nach Hause genommen werden soll.

Tulpenbuffet. In schlanke Glasvasen eingestellt, erhält das fragile Spiel der langstieligen Tulpen eine bessere Standfestigkeit. Die einzelne Tulpe ist dabei wie zuvor tütenartig umhüllt, indem sie in ein wassergefülltes Orchideenröhrchen gesteckt und dieses von der Papiertüte verdeckt wird. Jedes zweite Glas beinhaltet eine Kerze, die auf einer Metalltüte thront.
Um der übersteigerten, himmelwärtsstrebenden Dekoration einen optischen Halt zu geben, trägt jedes Glas ein kleines Blütenkränzchen. Auch Blütenbegleiter der Tulpe wie der hellgrüne Frühlings-Schneeball, der ebenfalls in der Tütenumhüllung steckt, schafft die optische Verbindung zum Buffet.

Zylindrische Gläser (Haymann), Gläser (Haans), Duftkerzen (Kayak)

Tulip buffet. Placed in slim glass vases, the fragile interplay of the tulips with their long stems is given more stability. Each individual tulip is again encased in a paper cones, this time to conceal their tiny glass tubes of water. Every second vase is alternated with a candle, standing regally on a metal cone. To give this over-the-top decoration additional optical balance, each vase bears a tiny floral wreath.
Another floral companion of the tulip, the light-green snowball sharing its paper cone, creates a connection to the buffet.

cylindrical glasses (Haymann), glasses (Haans), scented candles (Kayak)

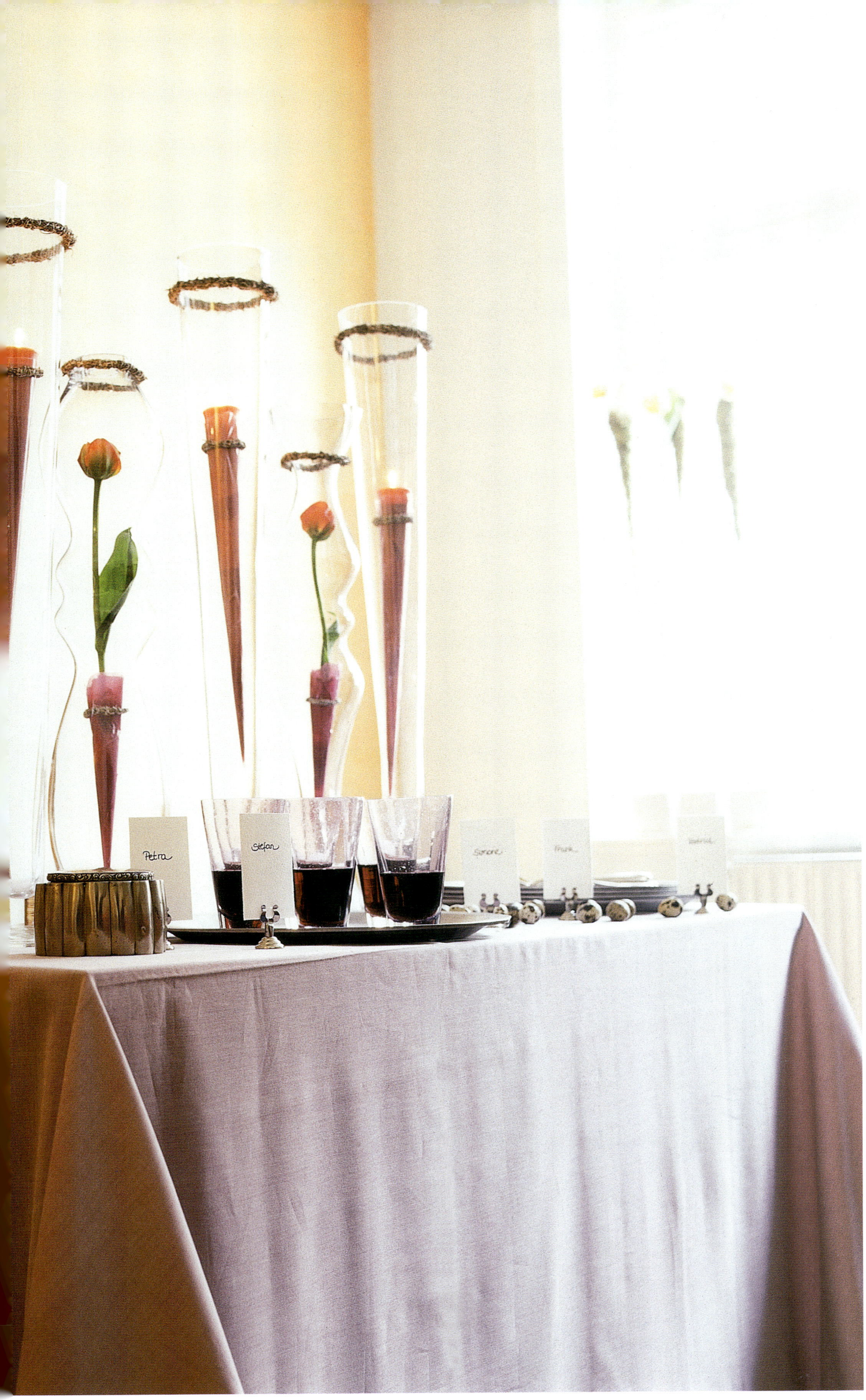
Petra
Stefan

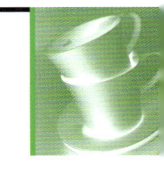

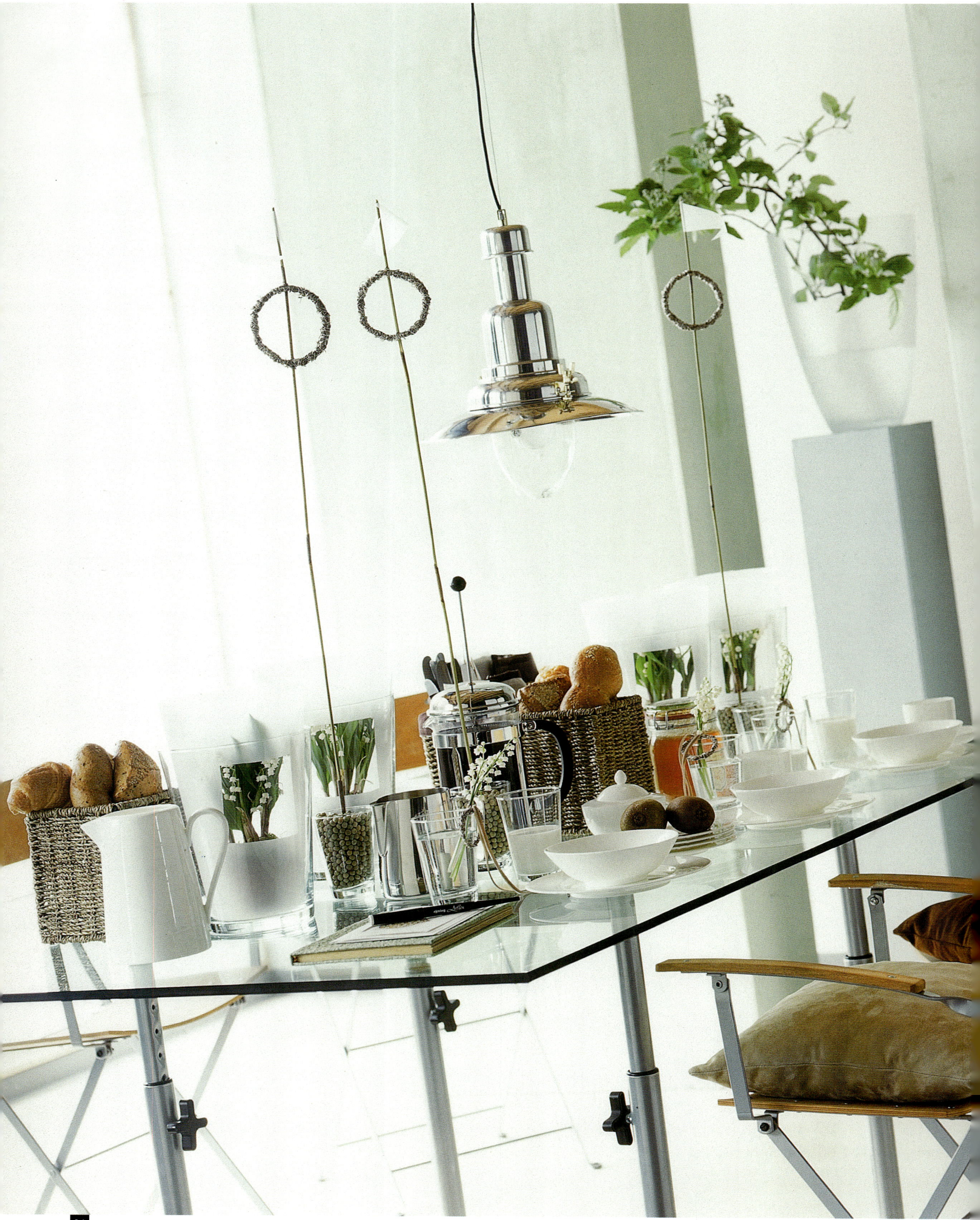

Mother`s Day breakfast
Muttertags-Frühstück

Überraschung nach dem Aufstehen. Der Tisch ist gedeckt, mit duftenden Brötchen, frischem Obst und gesunden Zutaten. Alles ist in das helle Morgenlicht getaucht und liebevoll mit kleinen Blütenakzenten versehen. Da macht der Tagesbeginn Spaß und Freude. Keine Pflanze symbolisiert die zärtliche Zuneigung und dankbare Liebe zu einem Menschen besser als das Maiglöckchen. Einzelne Pflanzen sind in transparente Glasgefäße gepflanzt, die den Blick auf ihre kostbaren wie kurzlebigen Blütenstängelchen freigeben.

Auch die übrige Tischdekoration hält sich farblich dezent im Hintergrund. Nichts drängt sich nach vorne, alles will zurückhaltend und bescheiden wirken. Eine liebliche Szenerie, die dabei Transparenz und Leichtigkeit ausstrahlt.

Bechergläser (Haymann), Service `Dibbern Bone` (Becker), Brotkörbe (Kayak), Tisch (Ikea), Stühle (Moulin Galland), Kissen (Hillo)

Surprise for Mom in the morning. The table is set with baskets of fresh rolls, fresh fruit and other healthy things. Everything is bathed in morning light and lovingly decorated with floral accents. What a wonderful way to begin a happy day!
No other plant can symbolize the tender affection and thankful love for another person like the lily of the valley. Single plants are set in transparent glass pots, leaving their precious stems open to view. The rest of the table decoration keeps discreetly in the background with its colours. Nothing crying for attention, every element is reserved and simple-looking. A loving scene with an aura of transparency and lightness.

glass cups (Haymann), `Dibbern Bone` dishes (Becker), bread baskets (Kayak), table (Ikea), chairs (Moulin Galland), cushions (Hillo)

Muttertags-Frühstück. Hier gilt das Prinzip: Weniger ist mehr. Einzelne Blütentriebe des Maiglöckchens sind zu zweit oder zu dritt mit einem Samtschleifchen an einen mit Silberdraht umwikkelten *Tillandsia*-Ring gebunden. Indem dieser außen am Glas platziert wird, gibt er den Stängeln den nötigen Halt am Rand des weiten Wasserglases. Eine gute Idee, wenn keine schmalen, dünnen Väschen zur Hand sind. Andererseits unterstreicht gerade diese vereinzelte Darstellung das Besondere der Maienblume. Und: Ein Mehr an Blüten würde auch ihren ohnehin intensiven Duft intensivieren, was am frühen Morgen eventuell des Guten zuviel sein könnte.

Mother's Day breakfast. The motto here: less is more. Delicate bunches of two or three single stems of lilies of the valley are encircled by a thin velvet ribbon and affixed to a *Tillandsia* ring with silver wire. This tiny bouquet is placed on the outside of a water glass, giving the stems the support they need to stand up. A good idea when there are no vases small enough at hand. At the same time, this individual representation underscores the special qualities of the lily of the valley. And more than just a few of these intensively-scented flowers would perhaps be too much of a good thing so early in the morning.

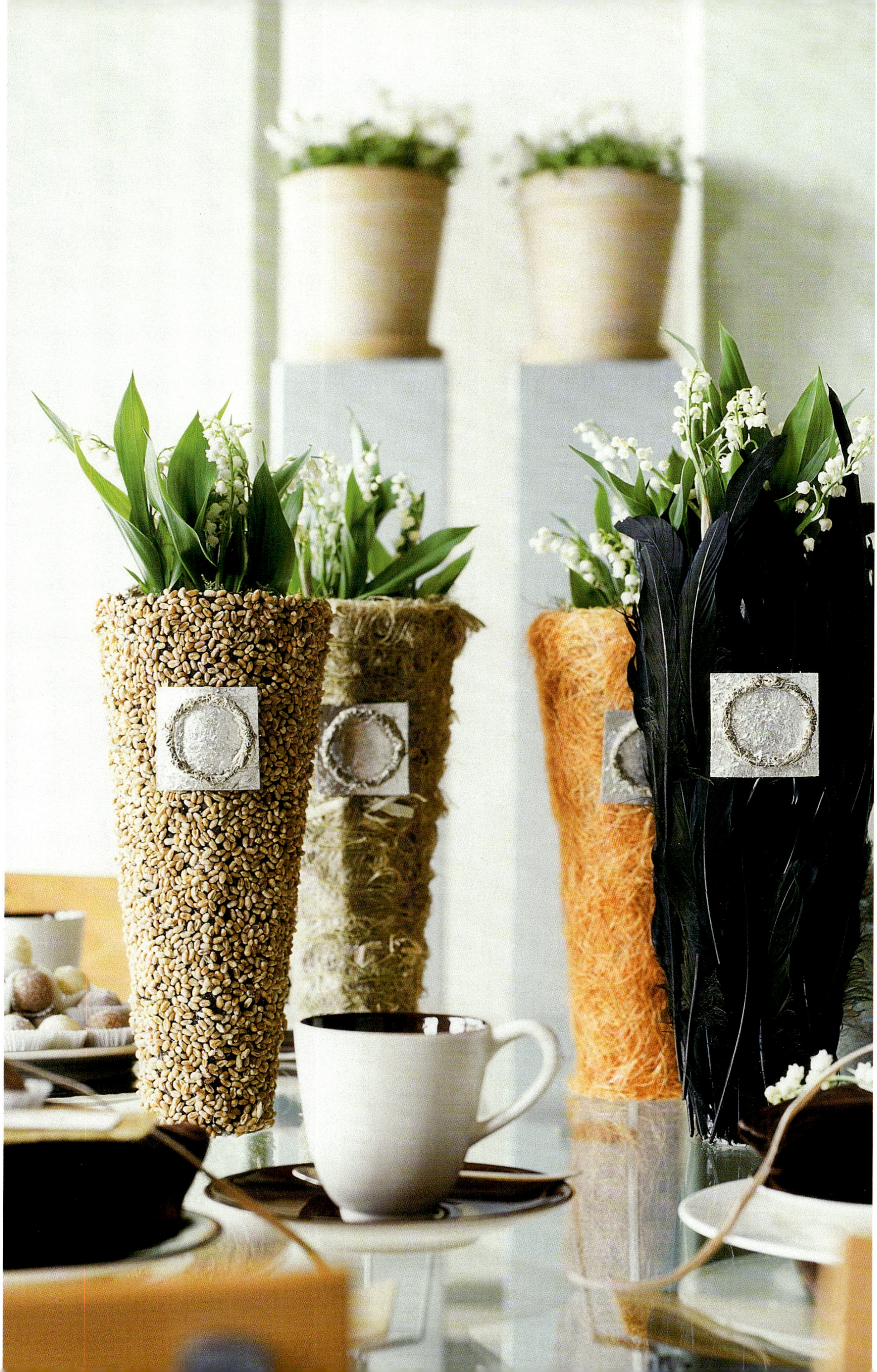

Muttertags-Frühstück. Wo das Kaffee-Service in Braun-Weiß daherkommt, muss auch der Blütendekoration einen markanteren Auftritt verschafft werden. Vor allem dann, wenn es um das zarte Maiglöckchen geht. Überproportioniert schlanke Töpfe geben ihr hier die Wertigkeit, die ihr zusteht. Als grüner Akzent mit den zarten, weißen Glöckchen-Rispen thronen sie über den mit Fasern, Körnern, Federn und Papieren ummantelten Gefäßen.
In gleichmäßiger Reihung oder im Karree aufgestellt, geben sie so den eindrucksvollen und ausdrucksstarken Schmuck ab.
Ein einzelner, blattversilberter Blütenstängel ziert die Platzkarte und das samtumwickelte Muttertagspräsent.

Mother`s Day breakfast. Such striking dishes in brown-and-white call for an equally unusual floral decoration. Especially when the lily of the valley is to be on centre stage. Oversized tapered pots create the mise en scène she deserves. As a green accent with her delicate, bell-shaped panicles, she sits on high atop a throne covered with natural fibres, grains and seeds, feathers and paper. Set in an even row or in a square formation, these pots make an impressive and expressive decoration. Individual silver-plated flowers adorn the place cards and the Mother`s Day present wrapped in velvet.

dishes (ASA), ribbons (Senn), serviettes (ASA), sisal fibres (Steingaesser), feathers (Pizarro)

Geschirr (ASA), Bänder (Senn), Servietten (ASA), Sisal (Steingaesser), Federn (Pizarro)

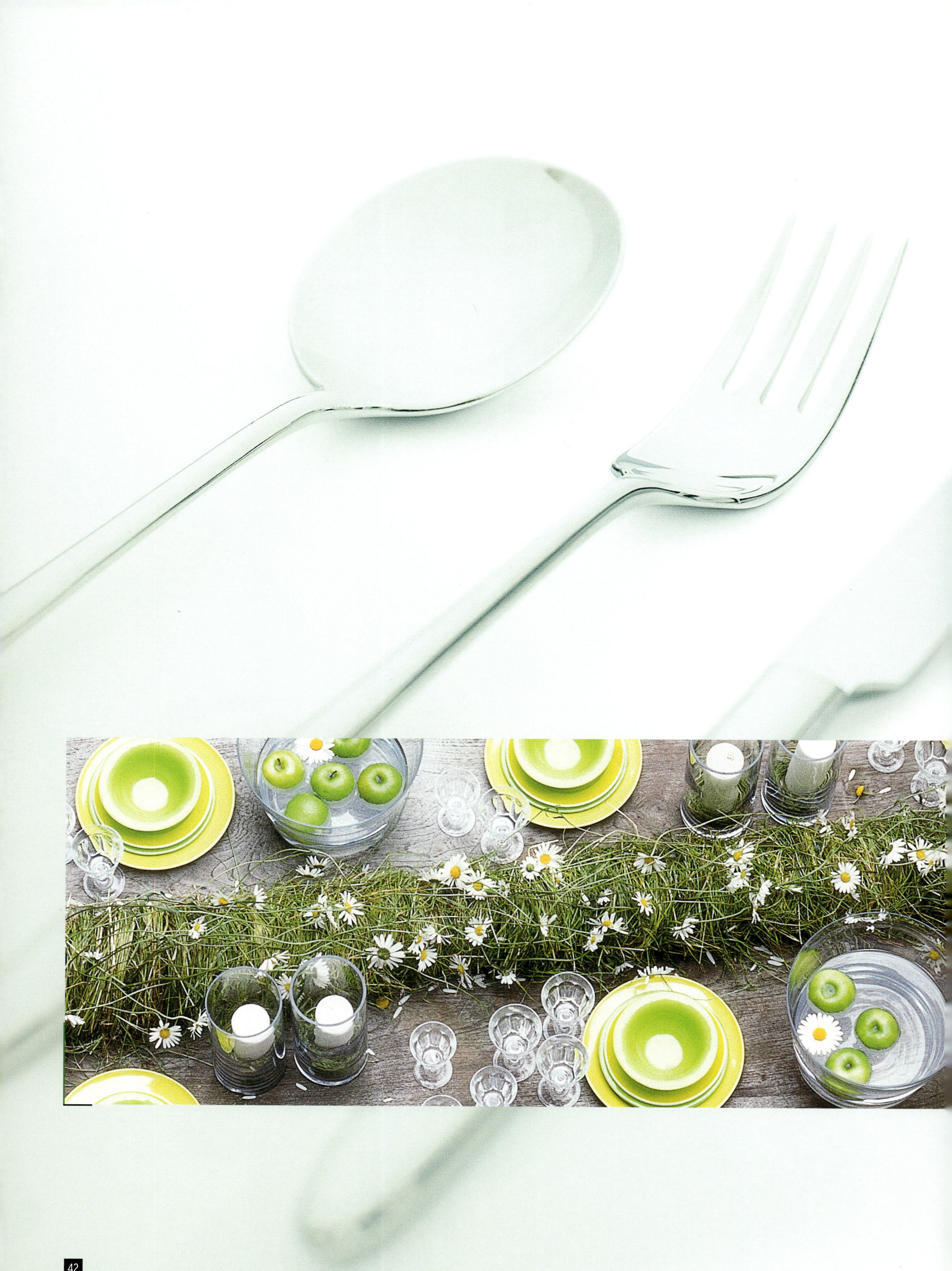

Summer Guests
SommerGäste

Summer garden
Sommergarten

Marguerite table
Margeritentafel

Summer dance
Sommerreigen

Solo players
Solistentreffen

Floral romance
Blütenromanze

SummerGuests
SommerGäste

Wer hat das noch nicht beobachtet, dass das helle Sonnenlicht im Sommer die Farben in einen ganz neuen Zauber hüllt? Das, was den Reiz und die einzigartige Atmosphäre in sonnenverwöhnten, mediterranen Ländern ausmacht, ist uns einige Monate auch gegönnt. Das Leben im Freien, unter dem blauen Himmel, den Wolken, den Sonnenstrahlen, unter dem Blätterdach der Bäume und umsäumt vom Grün der sommerlichen Vegetation bringt uns das richtige Sommerfeeling. Kein Wunder, dass jetzt die Feste draußen gefeiert werden, wo man laue Sommerabende plaudernd bei Kerzenschein verbringt und jegliche Geselligkeit ins „Grüne" verlagert. Die ersten Beeren, duftende Blumen, das saftige Grün der Wiesen, die belaubten Bäume bestimmen unsere Tischgestaltungen mit. Alles zeigt jetzt eine intensivere Farbigkeit.

Sommergarten, eine Tafeldekoration, die die Sinne betört. Die Sonne macht warmes Erdbeerrot zum Reinbeißen verführerisch und leuchtend-kühles Lavendelblau noch reiner.

Margeritentafel, eine frischgrüne Ode an den Sommer, die im Anschluß an einen Spaziergang durch Margeriten übersäte Wiesen ein ganz natürliches und sommerlich-vitales „Muss" ist.

Sommerreigen, warm-wirkende, tänzelnde Kerzenlichter in lauer Sommernacht lassen die Farben der Blumen fast unwirklich erscheinen. Eine besondere Farbfacette des Sommers.

Solistentreffen, bei dem Blau und Weiß im Mittelpunkt der Bühne stehen. Das schafft eine erfrischend kühle Wirkung. Der Sommer und blauer Rittersporn in ihrer reinsten Form.

Blütenromanze, die die Leichtigkeit des Sommers widerspiegelt. Weiße Akzente zähmen das intensive Rot mit seiner impulsiven, irisierenden Wärme.

Have you ever noticed how the bright sunlight on a summer`s day gives a totally new ambience to colours? The charm and unique atmosphere of sun-drenched Mediterranean lands is ours too – if only for a few short months each year. Outdoor living under a clear blue sky, the clouds, the rays of sunlight, under a leafy canopy of trees and surrounded by summer vegetation – all combine to give us that special summer feeling. It`s no wonder celebrations are held outside, where the guests can while away warm summer nights in the glow of candlelight with Mother Nature as hostess. The first berries, fragrant flowers, the moist green of meadows, and leafy cool trees all have an effect on our table creations. In this season everything shows more intensive colours.

Summer garden, a table decoration that dazzles the senses. The sunlight reflecting off strawberry red creates a seductive ambience and makes the cool lavender blue look even purer.

Marguerite table, a refreshing green ode to summer that is a natural "must" full of summery vitality, especially after a walk through meadows covered with marguerite daisies.

Summer dance, warm flickering candlelight on a mild summer night makes the colours of the flowers appear almost unreal. A special colour facet of summer.

Solo players, with the colours blue and white on centre stage for a refreshingly cool effect. Summertime and bright blue *Delphinium* in their purest form.

Floral romance, reflecting the lightness of summer. The white highlights tame the fiery red with its impulsive warmth.

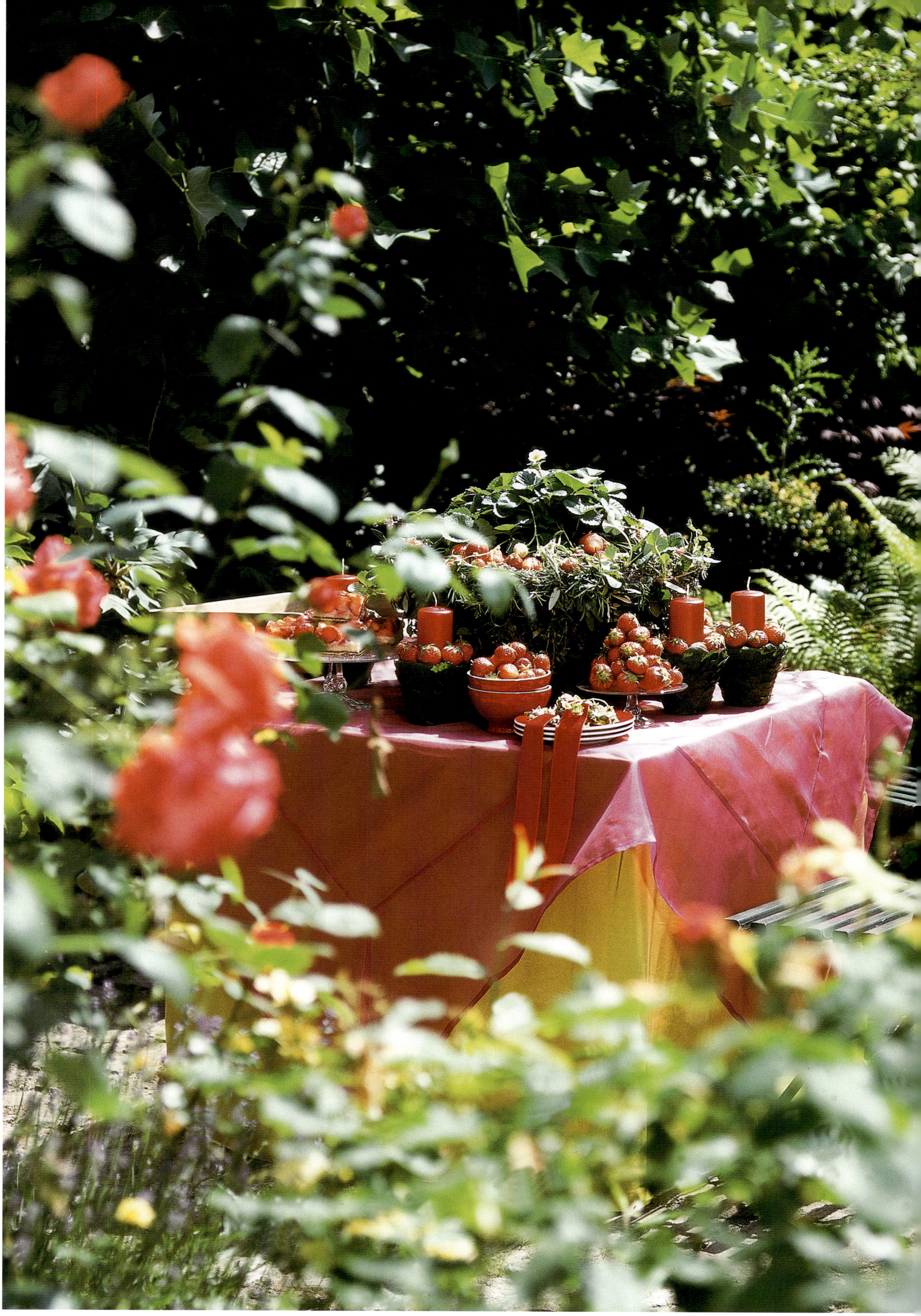

Summer garden

Sommergarten

Frühsommer – Erdbeerzeit. Kaum eine Beere symbolisiert mehr den beginnenden Sommer als die köstlichste aller Früchte, die Erdbeere. Geradezu eine sinnliche Wirkung wird ihr zugesprochen. Einerseits der roten Farbe, andererseits des hoch aromatischen Geschmackes wegen. Selbst Johann Wolfgang von Goethe erfreute seine Geliebte Charlotte von Stein mit frischen Erdbeeren. Es mag in dieser Saison kaum ein Gartenfest oder eine Kaffeetafel im Freien geben, bei der die Erdbeere nicht eine Rolle spielt. Geradezu wie ein sommerlicher Liebestraum wirkt es, wenn ihr sogar eine ganze Dekoration gewidmet ist – konsequent in den Farben Rot und Grün gehalten.

Early summer – strawberry season. Scarcely a berry symbolizes the coming of summer better than the most delicious of them all – the strawberry. An almost sensuous character is attributed to this fruit. For one, due to its sensual red colour, and also because of its aromatic flavour. Even Johann Wolfgang von Goethe was fond of presenting fresh strawberries to his beloved Charlotte von Stein. At this time of year, the strawberry is the star of the show at almost every garden party. An effect almost like a summery love scene is created when an entire table decoration is devoted to them – naturally keeping to the basic colours of red and green.

Kerzen (AV), Glasetagere (Veip), Tischtuch (Leupold)

candles (AV), glass cake plate (Veip), tablecloth (Leupold)

Sommergarten. Der Kräuterkorb gefüllt mit den frischen Erdbeerfrüchten ist der Mittelpunkt der Erdbeertafel.
Dazu ist Maschendraht schalenartig geformt und mit den frischen Trieben von *Oreganum*, Thymian, Salbei oder Rosmarin durchzogen worden. Damit auch das Erdbeerlaub und die Blüten in der Tischszenerie vorhanden sind, ist eine einzelne Erdbeerpflanze in einen Tontopf gepflanzt und ebenfalls eingestellt worden. Ausgepolstert mit Moos werden dann die frisch gewaschenen und zum unmittelbaren Naschen gedachten Früchte aufgefüllt. Die Teller der Tischgäste sind zusätzlich mit kleinen Kräuterkränzchen und rotem Samtband geschmückt.
Mit Sand gefüllte und außen mit Erdbeerlaub beklebte Tontöpfe dienen als Halterung für die erdbeerroten Stumpenkerzen. Der Topf kann mit Wachs überzogen und damit für einige Tage haltbar gemacht werden.

Summer garden. A herbal basket filled with fresh strawberries is the star of the show at this strawberry festival. Mesh wire is bent to form a bowl and woven and intertwined with fresh shoots of oregano, thyme, sage and rosemary. To complete the picture, a single strawberry plant with leaves and blossoms in a clay pot is placed in the basket. Next comes a soft bed of moss on which the freshly-washed and delicious-looking berries are piled. The plates of the table guests are additionally adorned with tiny herbal wreaths and red satin ribbons. Clay pots filled with sand and covered with rows of strawberry leaves serve as candleholders for the thick, berry-red candles. To keeps this decoration fresh for several days, the leafy jacket can be given a coat of wax.

49

Sommergarten. Um dem anbrechenden Sommer mit allen Sinnen zu begegnen, gehört neben einer liebevoll vorbereiteten Gastlichkeit und den köstlichen Gaumenfreuden auch der Blütenaugenschmaus dazu.
Wenn sich dann noch der betörende Duft hinzu gesellt, ist die Sommersinnlichkeit perfekt. Hier verzaubert Lavendel mit seinem Duft, der die Erinnerung an Wärme, Sonne, südlicher Lebensfreude mitschwingen läßt. Diese assoziierte Unkompliziertheit greift die schlichte und gleichermaßen faszinierende Tischdekoration auf. Einfache Gläser als Vasen sind mit Lavendel umwunden und roten, orangen und gelben Blumen gefüllt. Ein starker Farbkontrast, der die gesamte Leuchtkraft des Sommers herausstellt. Egal wie kurz oder lang die Tafel ist, solch eine einfache aber wirkungsvolle Blütenreihung kann unendlich fortgesetzt werden. Als Auflockerung dieser formalen Strenge werden einzelne Töpfe mit Lavendelpflanzen dazugestellt.
Einfach herzustellen sind auch die kleinen Präsente für jeden Gast. In Organzasäckchen sind Lavendelblüten gefüllt und mit Satinbändchen verknotet. Sie dienen als nette „Platzkarten" und beduften anschließend die Wäscheschubladen oder Kleiderschränke zuhause.

Summer garden. To better experience the approaching summer with all the senses, a floral feast for the eyes is the finishing touch for warm hospitality and lovingly prepared delicacies. Add to this the captivating scent of the flowers, and the sensuality of summer is complete. Here the bewitching perfume of lavender, reminiscent of warm sun and Mediterranean joie de vivre.

These associations of uncomplicated simplicity are taken up by the simple and fascinating table decorations. Plain glass tumblers covered with fragrant rows of lavender serve as vases, filled with red, orange and yellow flowers. A striking colour contrast which illustrates the luminosity of summer especially well. Depending on the length of the table, such a simple but effective row of floral arrangements can be added to infinitely. To break up the formal strictness, pots of lavender plants are placed here and there.

Also simple to make are the little presents for the guests. Organza pouches are filled with lavender flowers and tied with pretty satin ribbons. With their hand-written name tags these sachets also serve as name cards for the table. And after the party they will perfume linen cupboards or clothes closets.

Sektgläser, Glastablett (Veip), Bänder (Senn), Teelichtergläser (Kayak), Lavendel (Pinaruh)

champagne glasses, glass tray (Veip), ribbons (Senn), glasses for tea candles (Kayak), lavender (Pinaruh)

Sommergäste im Grünen. Auf dem langen, derben Holztisch mit der wiesigen Dekoration aus Gras und Margeriten kommt die ganze sommerliche Frische besonders gut heraus.

Sie ist so einfach herzustellen, dass sie sowohl im ländlichen Garten unter blühenden Apfelbäumen als auch beim Nachbarschaftsfest im städtischen Hinterhof verwirklicht werden kann. In der konsequenten Verwendung der Farben Apfel-Granny-Grün und strahlendem Weiß werden sich an dieser Sommertafel designgewöhnte Avantgardisten wie romantische Naturliebhaber wohlfühlen.

Summer guests out of doors. On a long, crude wooden table decorated with meadowy elements of grass and marguerite daisies, the freshness of summer comes across well. So easy to make, it is just as suitable for a country garden under blossoming apple trees as for a neighbourhood party in a city courtyard.

With the uniform arrangement of the colours – Granny Smith green and brilliant white – trendy avant-gardists and romantic nature lovers alike will feel at home.

Geschirr (Becker), Gläser (Veip),
Windlichter (Sandra Rich), Kerzen (AV)

dishes (Becker), glasses (Veip), hurricane lamps
(Sandra Rich), candles (AV)

Marguerite table
Margeritentafel

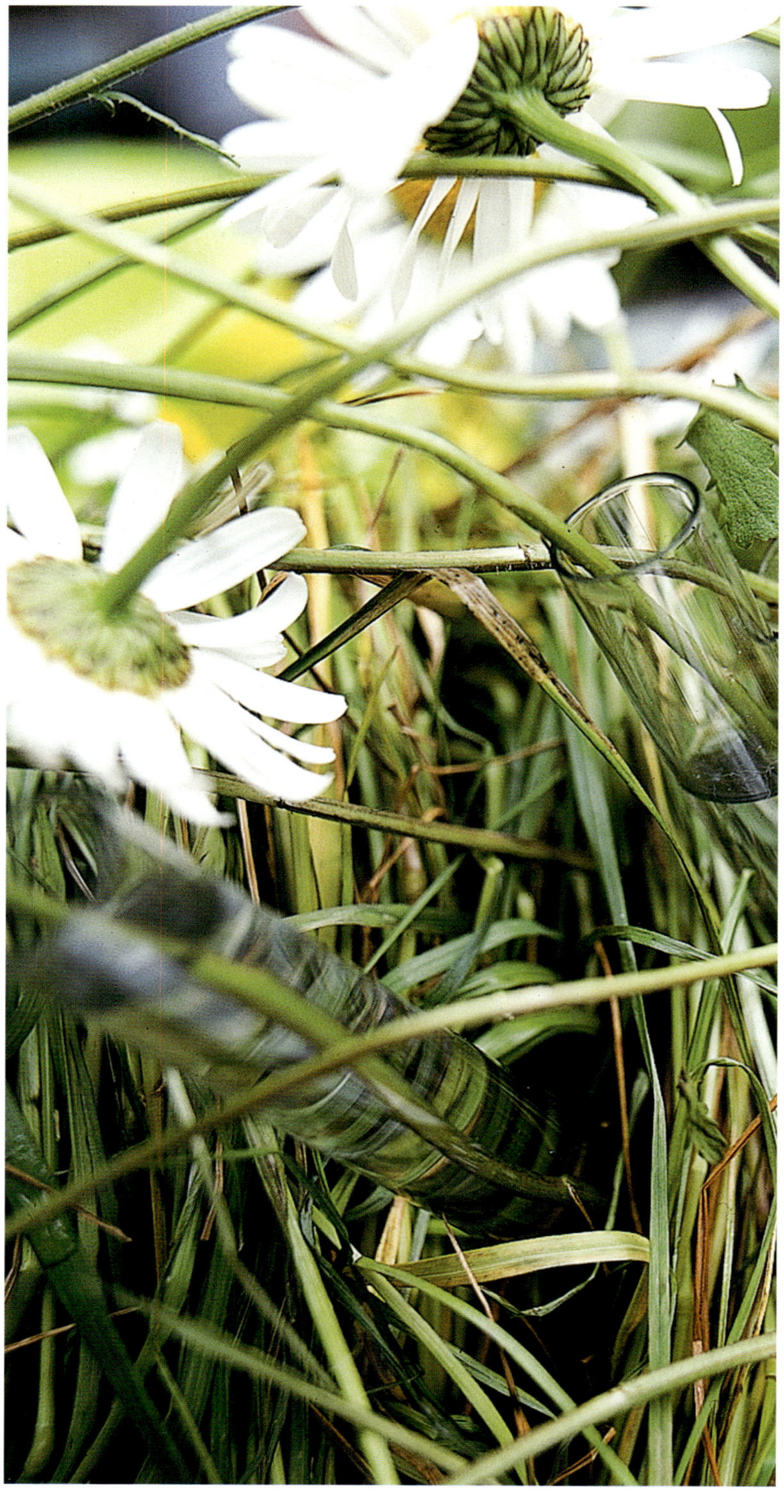

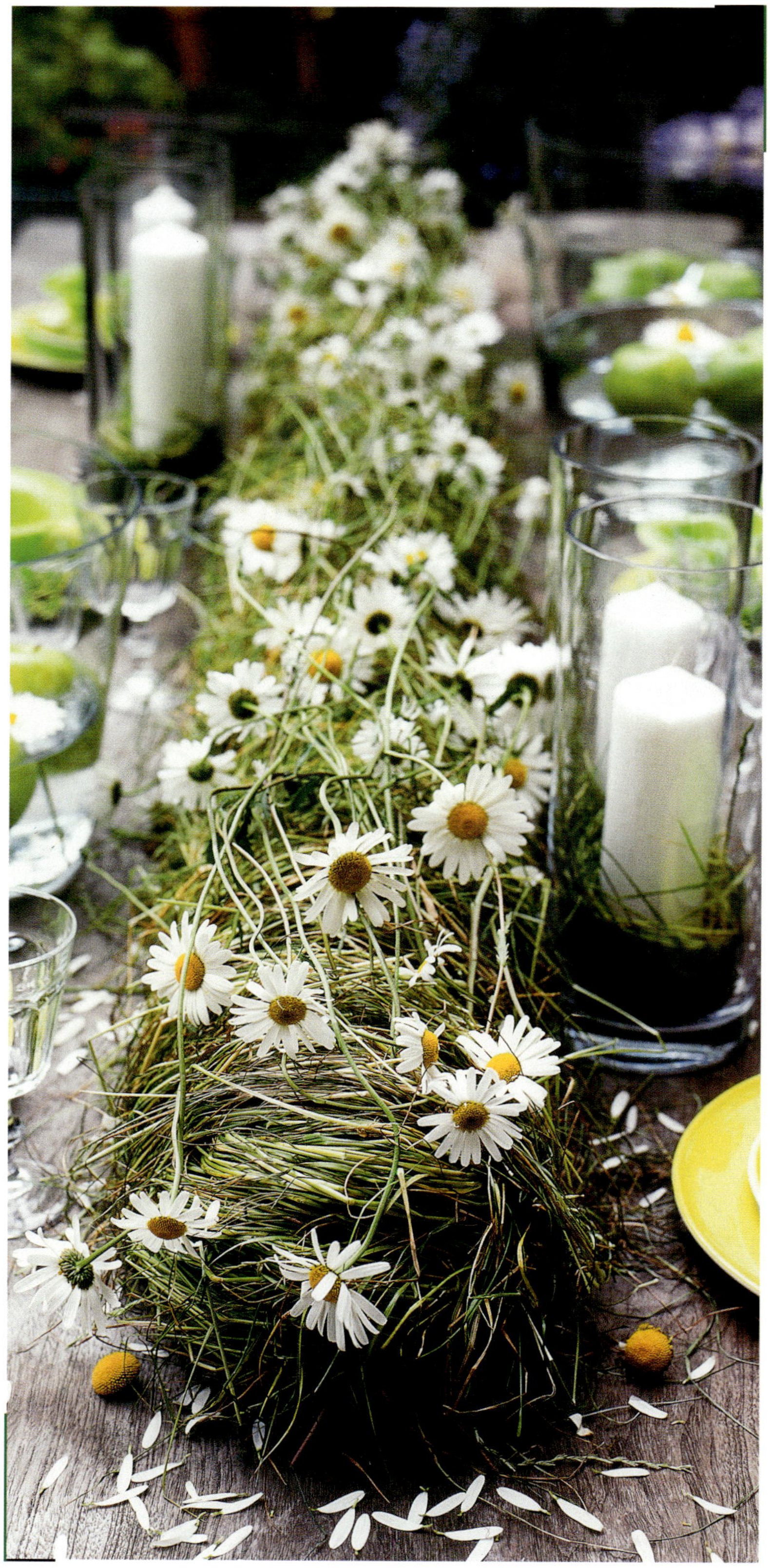

Margeritentafel. Die schöne Tischdekoration ist schnell zu erstellen. Eine Dachlatte wird mit angedrahteten Grasbüscheln dick umwickelt.
Wassergefüllte Reagenzgläser, die die Margeriten frischhalten, werden kreuz und quer einigermaßen regelmäßig verteilt eingesteckt. So entsteht eine natürliche, wie ästhetisch ansprechende Gestaltung. Auch die großen Stumpenkerzen in den Windlichtern sind passend mit Gras umwickelt.
Ganz raffiniert dazu werden die Serviettenringe aus den frischgrünen Fruchtblättern der *Lunaria*, des Silberpfennigs, gestaltet. Hier können beim Auffädeln auf stärkeren Draht alle Kinder tatkräftig mithelfen. Circa 12 Zentimeter sind notwendig, um zum Ring geformt und um die Serviette gelegt zu werden.

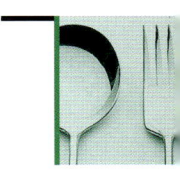

Marguerite table. This attractive table decoration is quick and easy to make. A length of rafter is wound about with a thick layer of wired grass tufts. Test tubes filled with water to keep the marguerite daisies fresh are inserted in a somewhat regular zigzag pattern. The result is a natural and aesthetically-pleasing arrangement. The thick candles in the hurricane lamps are also set in matching nests of grass.
An ingenious finishing touch are the serviette rings of fresh green *Lunaria*, or "silver dollars". Stringing the leaves onto the medium-weight wires is a job children love to help with. About 12 centimetres are needed to make a ring to fit around a rolled-up napkin.

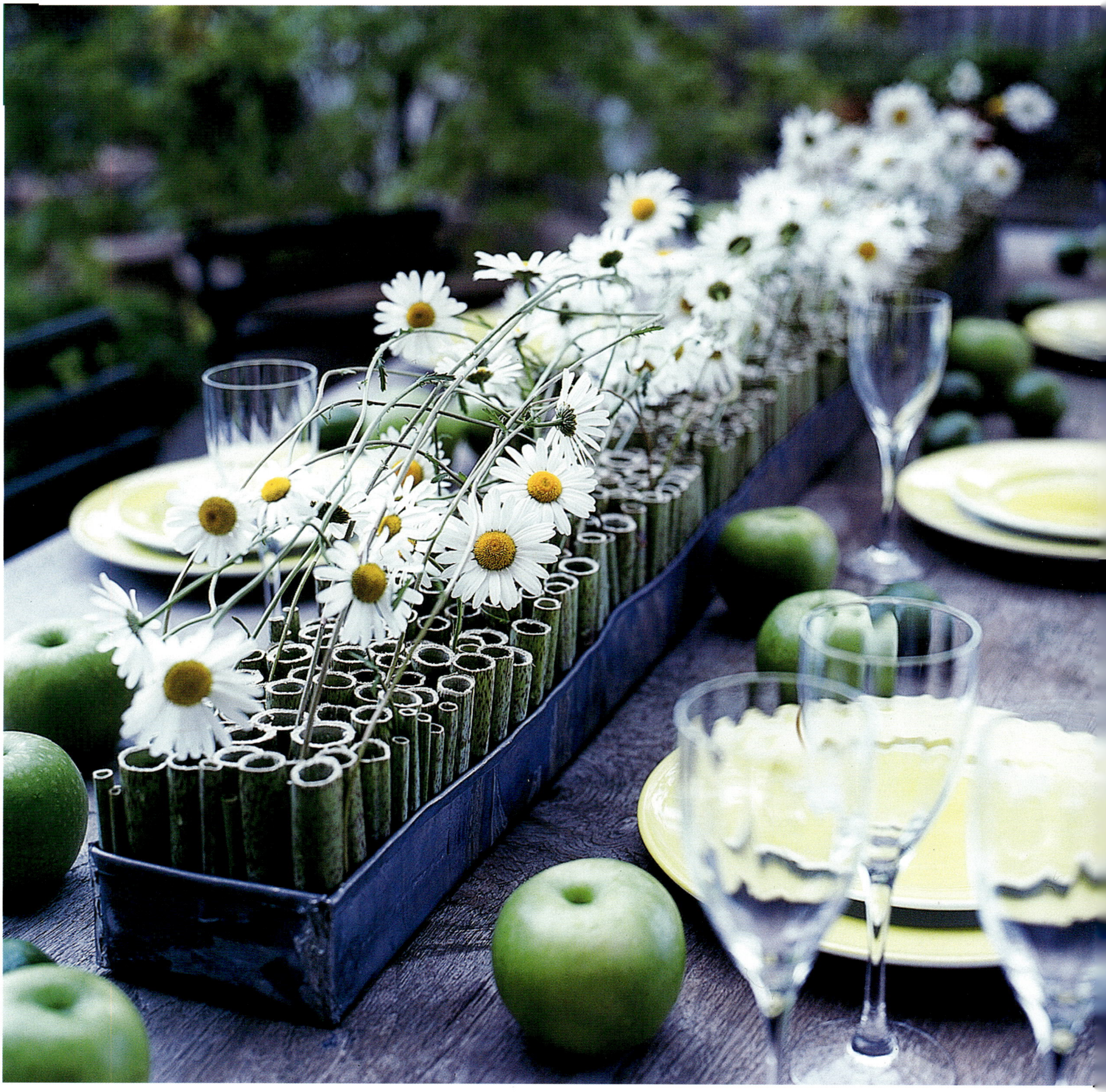

Margeritentafel. Wer bewußt im Sommer die Straßengräben und Waldränder beobachtet, wird die großen Stauden des schnellwachsenden Knöterichs ausmachen. Aus seinen grünen, hohlen Halmen lassen sich interessante Gestaltungen erstellen. Beispielsweise auch eine Alternative zu der eher unruhig und wiesig wirkenden Tafelgirlande aus Gras. Wer es eher grafisch-klar liebt, kann gleichlang geschnittene Halmabschnitte senkrecht in eine rechteckige Walzbleiwanne schichten. Diese ist individuell entsprechend der Tischlänge zu formen. Die Stirnseiten werden verlötet, die Längskanten zur besseren Stabilität umgeschlagen. Ist die Wanne nicht ganz wasserdicht, wird zusätzlich mit Silikon abgedichtet. Daraufhin werden die Margeriten kreuz und quer in Längsrichtung der Tafel in die Halmabschnitte gesteckt. Das i-Tüpfelchen der Tafelgestaltung sind die Tischkarten, die an den Halmen befestigt sind.

Geschirr (Becker), Walzblei (Dachdecker)
dishes (Becker), sheet lead (Dachdecker)

Marguerite table. Anyone who closely watches the ditches along the side of the road and bordering forests in summer will notice the hardy stocks of the fast-growing *Polygonum* grass. One can make the most interesting creations with its hollow green stems.
For example, as an alternative to the otherwise wild and meadowy table garland of grass. If you prefer things to be more symmetrical, the tubes can be lined up in even rows in a rectangular metal trough, the length of which is determined individually by the size of the table. The front ends are welded together while the sides are folded down for better stability. If the trough is not completely waterproof, it can be lined additionally with silicon. Then the marguerite daisies can be inserted into the tubes along the length of the table. The final detail of this jolly table arrangement is in the matching name cards, which are attached with gold wire to short lengths of the green tubes.

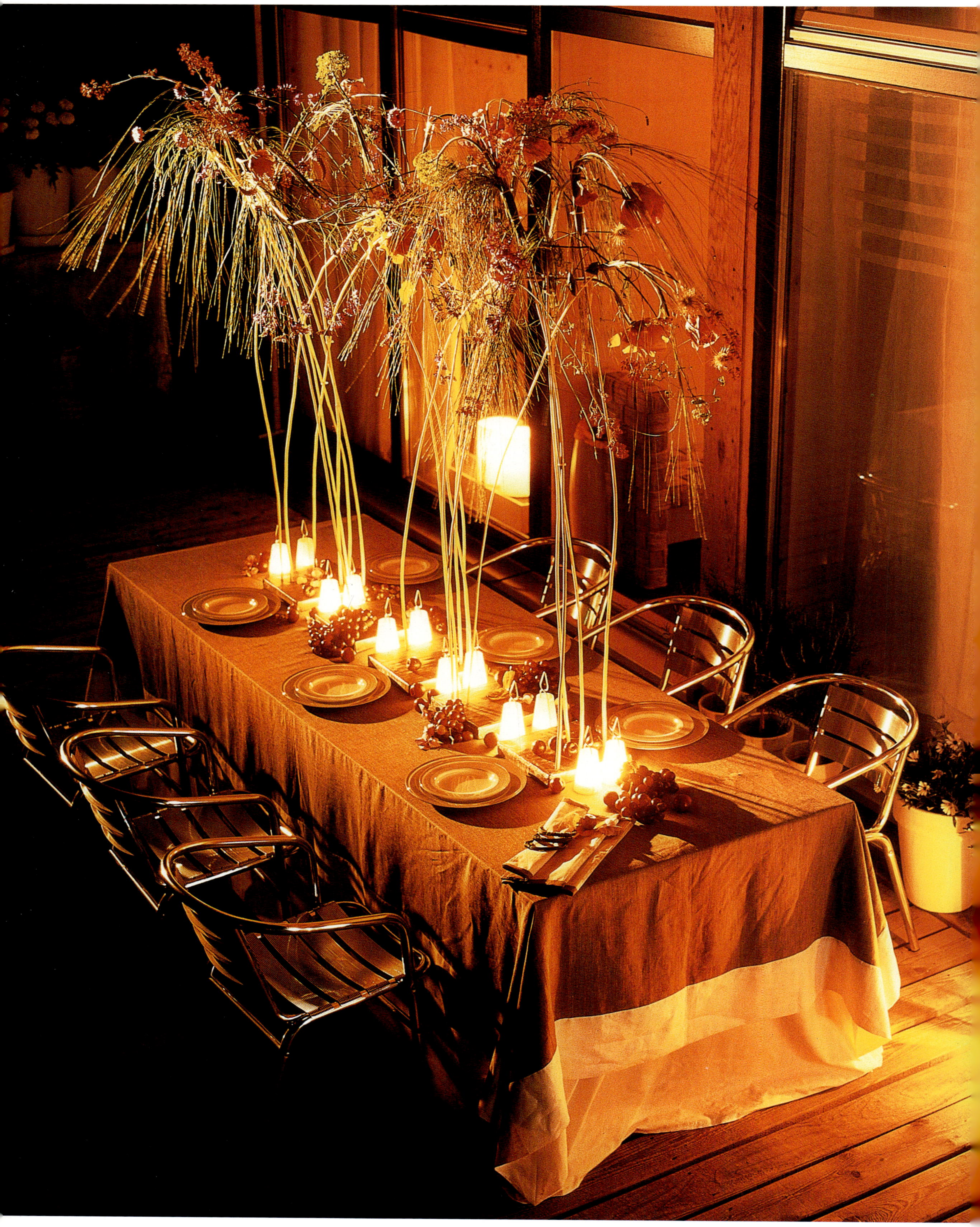

Summer dance
Sommerreigen

Stühle (Ikea), Laternen (Drescher), Tischwäsche (Haymann), Geschirr (Leupold), Windlichter (Hakbijl)

chairs (Ikea), lanterns (Drescher), table linen (Haymann), dishes (Leupold), hurricane lamps (Hakbijl)

Blütenbaldachin. Über den Tisch hinweg durch die Blume sprechen zu müssen, kann den geladenen Gästen das lebhafte Miteinander schnell verleiden. Blickkontakt ist für eine amüsante, unterhaltsame Einladung zu Tisch ebenso wichtig, wie die besonderen Speisen. Da dürfen also auch die Blumen nicht stören. Insofern sollte der Schmuck entweder unterhalb der Augenhöhe angebracht sein, oder aber er kann über den Köpfen der Gäste schweben und damit geradezu einen Blütenbaldachin bilden. Eine schöne Idee ist es, die Blüten und Rispen auf Stelzen sich zueinander hin neigend anzuordnen. Ein Sommerblütendach, das besonders beim abendlichen Fest unter freiem Himmel eine farbenfrohe, stimmige Umrahmung schafft.

Floral baldachin. Having to talk through floral table decorations can quickly spoil the lively repartee between guests. A direct line of vision is just as important for an amusing and entertaining dinner party as the special gourmet delights served. The flowers should decorate, not irritate. Therefore the decorations should either stand at a height just under eye level or tower above the heads of the guests, creating a floral canopy over the table. A nice effect is also created when the flowers and panicles are placed leaning towards each other on stilts. A summery floral canopy for creating a colourful and lively atmosphere, especially for dining outside under the stars.

Summer dance. Wicker poles inserted into a square base overlaid with metal hold aloft glass tubes for the flowers. On their long stems, the blooms swing gaily in all directions, creating an irregular but harmonious atmosphere. This leaves extra space on the table for fruit as well as groups of hurricane lamps. Especially when darkness falls, they lend a warm glow of candlelight to the party. A matching accessory: the clothespins overlaid with silver plate. Reflecting the candlelight, they also hold the names of the guests on scrolls of parchment paper. The serviette rings are made of wound grass.

Sommerreigen. Weidenstäbe, die in quadratische, mit Walzblei verkleidete Platten gesteckt werden, tragen am oberen Ende Glasröhrchen für die Blüten.
An ihren langen Stängeln schwingen diese in alle Richtungen unregelmäßig aber sehr harmonisch wirkend aus. So bleibt die übrige Tischfläche frei, um neben Obst zahlreiche Windlichter zu platzieren. Bei einbrechender Dunkelheit verleihen sie allem eine warme Kerzenstimmung.
Passend die blattvergoldeten Wäscheklammern. Sie reflektieren den Lichterschein und fixieren gleichzeitig die auf Pergament geschriebenen Namen der Geladenen.
Die Serviettenringe sind aus Gras gewunden.

Sommerreigen. Manchesmal ist zum einen eine flache Tischdekoration geeigneter; zum anderen Masse einfach nur klasse! In der Mengenbetonung der Gestaltung verliert das Einzelne zugunsten der fülligen Gesamtwirkung seine Individualität. Ob aus zahlreichen Wassergläsern, die jeder zuhause in seinem Küchenschrank stehen hat, oder aus trendigen Kunststoff-Väschen gestaltet: So eine Tischdekoration ist schnell und einfach zu bewerkstelligen und verblüfft die Gäste. Die Vasen können mit allerlei sommerlichen Blüten und Gräsern aus Garten, Wiese und Feldrain bestückt werden. Oder auf dem Heimweg wird ein dicker Arm voll Mohn oder Rosen beim Gärtner oder Floristen um die Ecke geholt. Da braucht es keine große Erfahrung, wie ein Strauß zu binden und in die Vase einzustellen ist. Die Blumen in gleiche Länge schneiden und bunt durcheinander in die bereits mit Wasser gefüllten und in der Tischmitte zusammengestellten Gefäße stecken. Die Geleekerzen bringen dann bei anbrechender Nacht zusätzlich Sommernachtsstimmung.

Summer dance. Sometimes a flat table decoration is the right thing, and other times extravagance is simply excellence! With the emphasis on excess, the individuality of the various elements steps aside to create perfection in profusion. Either with plain water glasses like we all have at home in our kitchen cupboards or trendy plastic vases, this table decoration is quick and easy to create and yet makes a lasting impression on the guests. The vases can be filled with all kinds of summer flowers and grasses from the garden, meadows and along fields. Or an armful of poppies or roses can be gathered on the way home, at a garden centre or from the florist`s around the corner. A lot of experience in binding bouquets and arranging them in vases is not necessary. Simply cut the stems to around the same length and mix them together in the glasses after these have been filled with water and placed closely together in the centre of the table. The jelly candles add a midsummer night atmosphere after dusk.

Kunststoffvasen (Kayak), Geleekerzen (Haymann), Geschirr (Becker)

plastic vases (Kayak), jelly candles (Haymann), dishes (Becker)

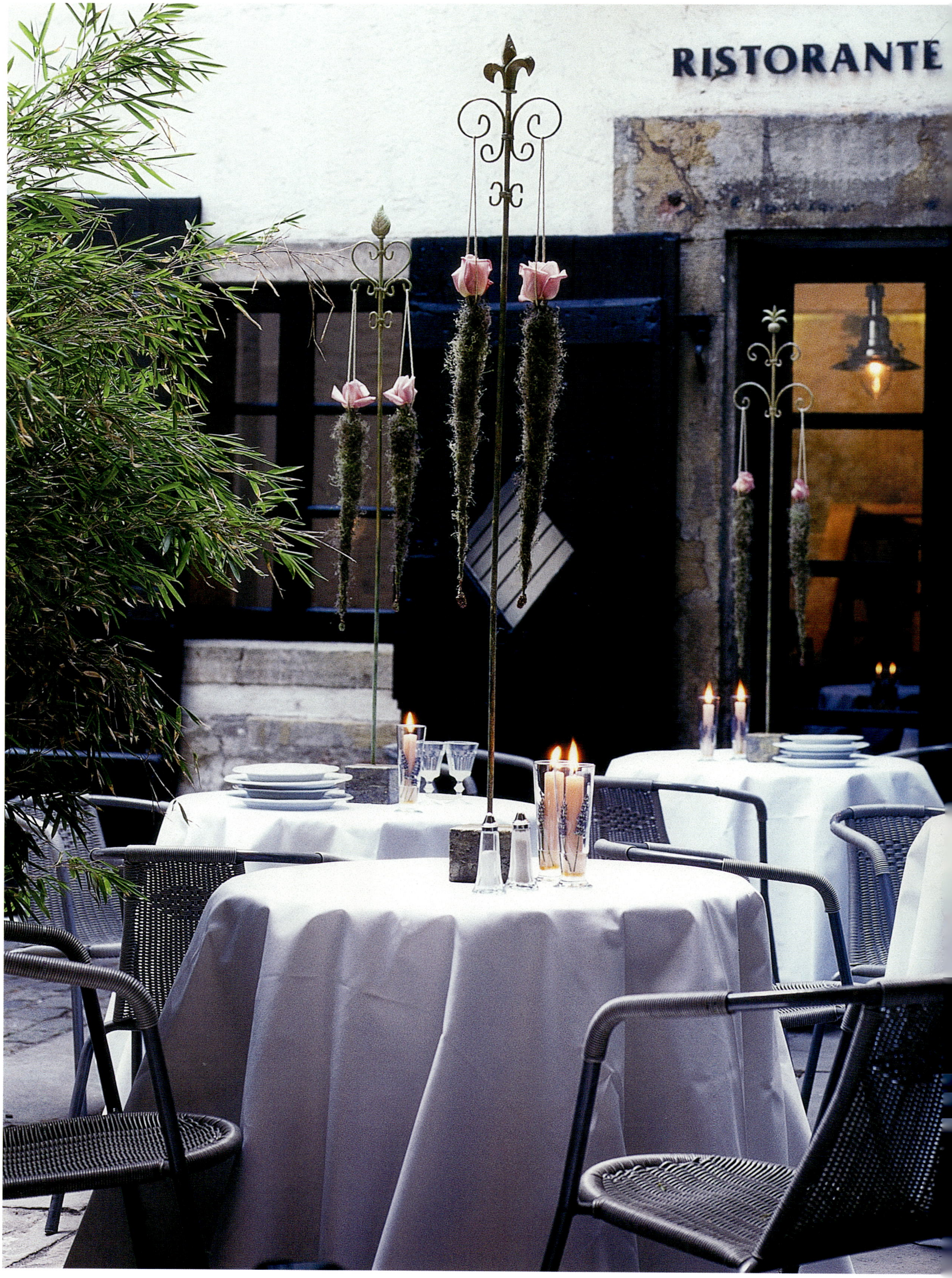
RISTORANTE

Solo players
Solistentreffen

Hommage an Bella Italia. Wenn es mal ganz besonders zugehen soll und der Tisch nicht allzu viel Platz für eine aufwendige Blütendekoration bereithält, strebt diese einfach hoch hinauf. Rosen in schmale Floraltüten gehängt, die von hohen Zierstäben hinabhängen, sind eine ausgefallene und aufmerksamkeitsstarke Lösung.
Damit verblüfft man sicher auch den Patrone, der trotz unschlagbar kulinarischer Speisenkarte oft nicht das Feeling für die Tischblumen hat. Außerdem haben darunter die köstlichen Frutti-di-mare-Platten und die vielen Wein- und Wassergläser auch noch Platz.

A tribute to bella Italia. When something extra special is needed and the table does not offer a lot of space for large and extravagant floral decorations, these roses are high flyers. Hanging on high in narrow floral cones which are suspended from thin decorative hooks, these roses can make a striking and unusual impression. Enough to astound even the padrone who, although he may offer an excellent gourmet menu, sometimes does not have the right feeling for table decorations. And besides, there is sure to be plenty of room left on the table for the delicious frutti di mare platter and the many wine and water glasses.

Gläser (Veip), Kordel (Halbach), Spalierstab (Florholz)

glasses (Veip), cord (Halbach), spalier pole (Florholz)

Solistentreffen. Mit etwas Vorbereitung ist eine Grundausstattung für eine Tischdekoration geschaffen, die jederzeit – auch mit anderen Blüten bestückt – Wiederverwendung finden kann. Ein quaderförmiger Pflasterstein wird angebohrt und mit einem Spalierstab versehen. Handelsübliche Orchideenröhrchen werden mit Maschendraht ummantelt und mit Hilfe von Sprühkleber mit sommerlichen Fruchtständen verziert. Wer keine Windlichter hat, macht sich welche. Die Stabkerzen werden mit Knetmasse in hohen Biergläsern fixiert und mit Lavendelblüten verziert. Die handgeschriebene Speisenkarte für dieses besondere Sommerfest wird mit Lavendelkränzchen und getrockneten Blättern geschmückt.

Windlichter (Hakbijl), Papier (Pulsar)
hurricane lamps (Hakbijl), paper (Pulsar)

Solo players. With a little advance preparation the basics are ready for a table decoration that can be used again and again, with different kinds of flowers. A small hole is drilled in the centre of a cobblestone and an espalier pole is inserted. Commercially bought orchid tubes are wrapped around with mesh wire and with the help of spray glue are covered with summery seed pods. If there are no hurricane lamps available, no problem – they are easy to make. The candlesticks are anchored with putty in tall beer glasses and decorated with lavender flowers.
The hand-written menu for this special summer party is adorned with miniature wreaths of lavender and dried leaves.

67

Solistentreffen. Schau mir in die Augen, Kleines... trotz der hohen 'Casablanca'-Lilie ist das hier kein Problem. Diese ist so über den Tischgästen schwebend angebracht, das sie zwar mit ihrem Duft betört, aber den Blickkontakt für das lukullische Tete-à-Tete keineswegs stört. Wie zuvor beschrieben, wird hier der Stab mit der Kunststoffgrabvase versehen, die mit Blattgold und Wachs eine edle Oberfläche erhalten hat. Das kaschiert elegant ihre ursprüngliche Bedeutung. Gleichzeitig bietet sie Platz für den Wurzelballen der *Lilium*-Pflanze. Die Basis wird mit Lavendelblüten und Bändern dekoriert.

Solo players. Here's lookin' at you kid ... despite the tall 'Casablanca' lilies this is not a problem here. The lily holds such a lofty position that, although still able to bewitch the guests with her perfume, she will not disturb the cosy tête-à-tête in any way. As already described, the top of the staff is fixed to a plastic cemetery vase, which has been given a luxurious coating of gold plate and wax, an elegant way to conceal its original purpose. At the same time there is room inside for the roots of the lily plant. The base is decorated with tiny bouquets of lavender blossoms and ribbons.

Kordel (Halbach), Organzaband (Vaban), Serviettenbrosche (Florholz), Schale (Kehrle), Gefäß (Des Pots), Etagere (Hakbijl)

cord (Halbach), organza ribbon (Vaban), serviette broach (Florholz), dish (Kehrle), pot (Des Pots), plate rack (Hakbijl)

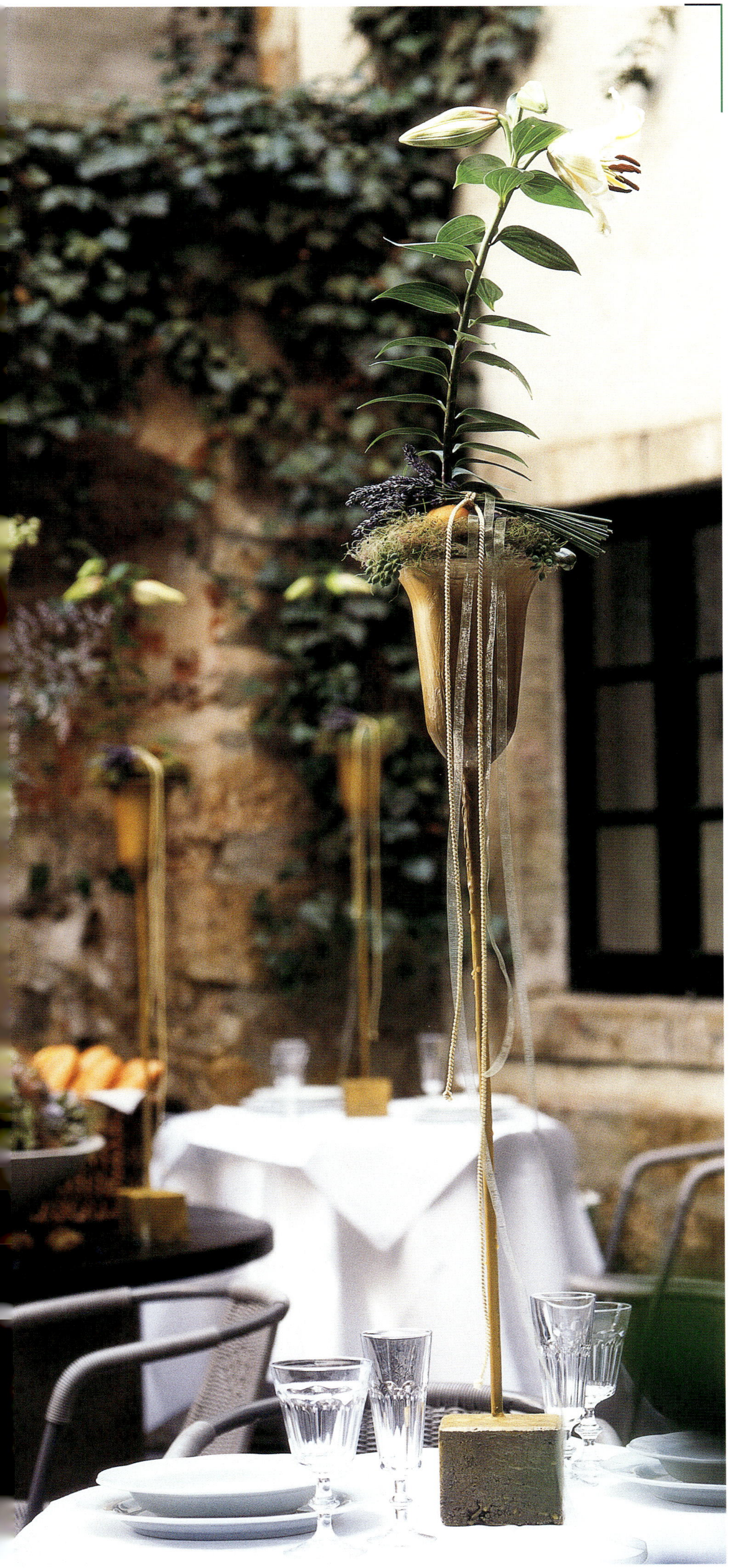

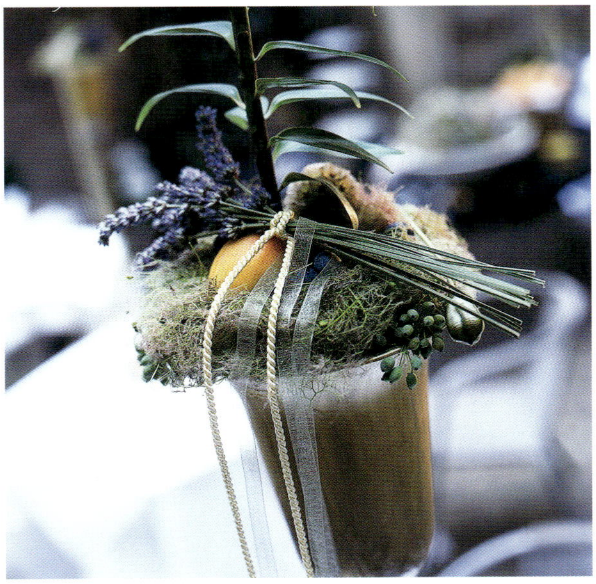

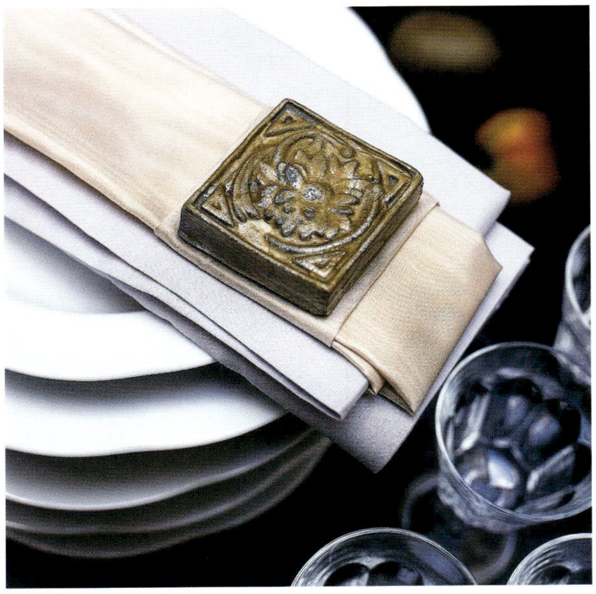

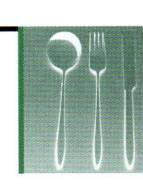

When standard floral decorations are intended to reflect the fine art of dining, these glass tubes with their spiral-shaped supports are trump over the run-of-the-mill porcelain vases. And that's not all. Allowed to show their graceful long stems now, the flowers can begin their solo dance. This is the contemporary alternative for table decorations that need to be stylish and also quick to make.
And when more friends join up and the table gets longer and longer, these sure-footed floral soloists can be multiplied to your heart's content to make a lively Polonaise procession.

Floral romance
Blütenromanze

Wo auch der Standard-Blütenschmuck das Spiegelbild der feinen Tischart sein soll, trumpfen jetzt die Reagenzröhrchen in Spiraldrahthalterung über die null-acht-fünfzehn Porzellanväschen auf. Und damit nicht genug. Die Blüten dürfen jetzt, ihre stattliche wie grazile Länge zeigend, hier ihren Solotanz vollbringen.
Das ist die zeitgemäße Alternative für Tischblumen, wenn's schnell und „stiel"voll sein soll. Und dennoch strahlt diese Gestaltung Stil und Wertigkeit aus.
Und wenn die Tafelrunden geselliger, die Tischreihung immer länger wird, dann stellen sich auch die standfesten Blumensolisten zur beliebig verlängerbaren Polonaise auf.

Reagenzröhrchen mit Fuß (Haymann),
Metallblätter (Kayak), Gläser (Haans)

glass tubes with stands (Haymann),
silver leaves (Kayak), glasses (Haans)

Floral romance. And when the fine art of dining dictates that the guests be greeted in the entrée with a fitting floral arrangement, this elegant summery creation at eye level will fit the bill. *Delphinium* are placed in a conical clay pot and arranged accurately to underscore the conversely proportional shape of the pot. The tiny glass vases for the individual table decorations fit perfectly in their plaster cube stands, and can easily be taken out to clean in the dishwasher. Water glasses filled with duckweed at each place setting create colourful and lively accents.

Blütenromanze. Wo die hohe Tischkunst mit dem eleganten Blütengespann bereits im Entrée die Gäste entsprechend blütenreich empfangen soll, bietet sich eine sommerlich-füllige Dekoration in Augenhöhe an. Rittersporn ist akkurat in einen konischen Tontopf gesteckt und greift damit die umgekehrt proportionale Gefäßform auf. Die kleinen Glasröhrchenvasen für die einzelnen Tischdekorationen stecken in Gipswürfeln, aus denen sie leicht entnommen und in der Geschirrspülmaschine gereinigt werden können. Mit Wasserlinsen gefüllte Gläser setzen in der Anzahl der Tischgäste farbige wie stimmungsvolle Akzente.

Bleisäulen (Kehrle), Schwimmkerzen (AV)
lead pillars (Kehrle), floating candles (AV)

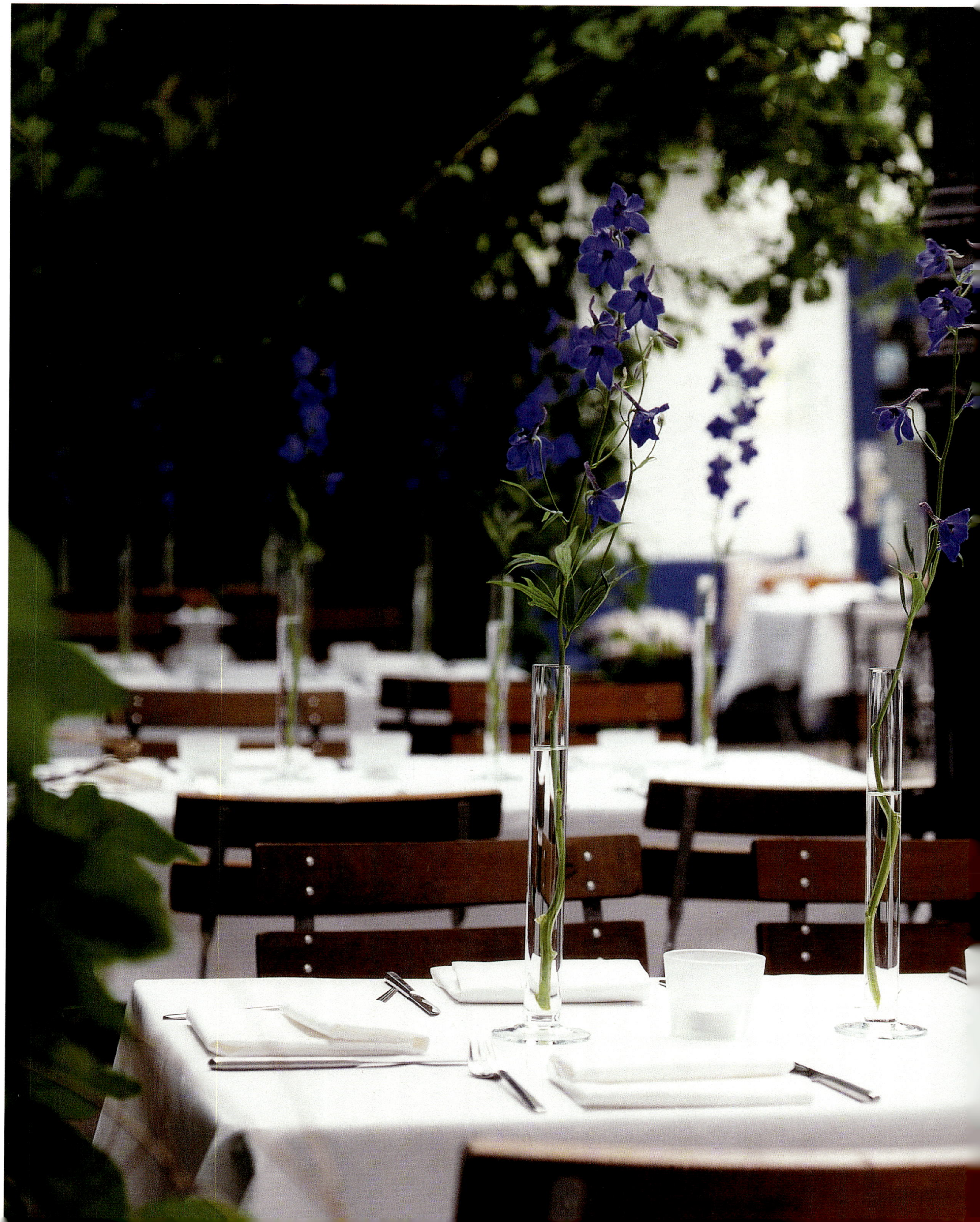

Blütenromanze. Wo die Blüten vielgestaltig sind, kann die Gestaltung entsprechend einfach sein. Und diese ist an Schlichtheit kombiniert mit eleganter Ausstrahlung kaum zu überbieten.

Moderne Glaszylinder machen's möglich. Sie sind eine praktische und schnelle Lösung, um Tische variabel und immer wieder effektvoll zu schmücken. Vor allem wenn es eine große Festgesellschaft gibt, die im Freien an langen Tischen feiert, ist ein Blütenschmuck auf Säulen passender als ein Zuviel auf den Einzeltischen. So hat jeder Gast Platz für Speisen, Getränke und ein direktes Gegenüber. Und bei jedem Gang zum Buffet oder zur Bar erfreut der flankierende Blütenschmuck auf hohen Säulen.

Floral romance. When more complex flowers are used, the decoration itself can be kept relatively simple.
And this one is hard to top for its combination of simplicity and elegance. The most modern glass cylinders make it possible. They are a practical and quick solution for decorating a table with a stunning effect every time. Particularly when a big party is planned on long tables out of doors, a very distinguished floral arrangement on its own special pedestal is more fitting than on the individual tables. This gives the guests more room for food and drink, as well as a direct vis-à-vis. And every time they pass by on the way to buffet or bar, everyone will be captured anew by the charm of the floral decorations on tall pillars.

*Glaszylinder (Sandra Rich),
Teelichtgläser (Florissima)*

*glass cylinders (Sandra Rich),
glasses for tea candles (Florissima)*

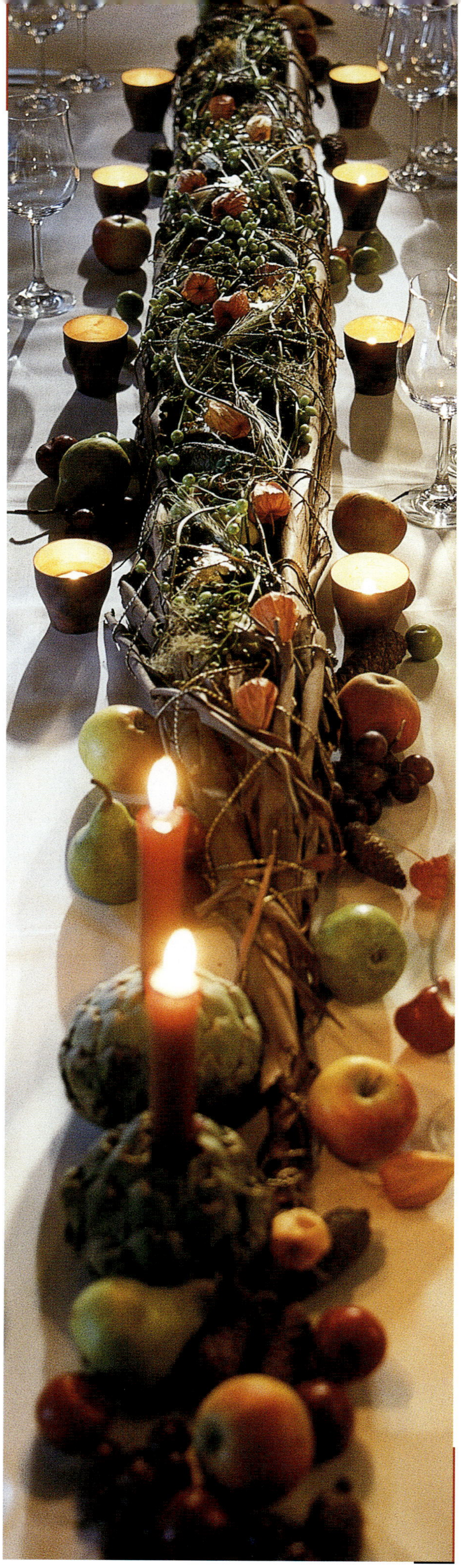

AutumnFestivities
HerbstFeste

Engagement party in perfect form
Formvollendete Verlobung

Jubilee in resplende...
Farb...

Classic wedding
Klassische Hochzeit

Sweet and charming baptism
Liebliche Taufe

Celebrating festive occasions. Although not strictly reserved for autumn, this season gives parties a particularly opulent character. The entire spectrum of floral colours is now at its zenith. Mother Nature flaunts her leaves in every thinkable nuance, and harvest baskets are filled to bursting with the rich and resplendent bounty of fruits.

This allows for superb celebrations – especially since table decorations can draw from the abundance of the horn of plenty in every sense of the word. The interplay of tones becomes a fireworks of forms and colours. But it is no less a challenge to create a peaceful, focused and worthy background for the festive occasion while restricting the colours to a minimum. Every idea can be altered slightly to be used again for another season. For example, instead of the autumny *Chrysanthemums*, tulips could be used in spring, or roses in summer. Nothing should be regarded as static; more important is an intuitive feeling for underlining the festivities with flowers.

Classic wedding, a table decoration reserved in its choice of colours, which draws a second glance to the greens and many other interesting elements.

Engagement party in perfect form, in violet brightened by white flowers as well as grey and silver elements, which

ours
ächtiges Jubiläum

AutumnFestivities

HerbstFeste

Birthday party full of atmosphere
Stimmungsvoller Geburtstag

create a youthful and easy-going atmosphere.

Sweet and charming baptism, roses and all kinds of sweet little blossoms make clear what joyful occasion is being celebrated. Delicate colour nuances to honour the birth of the child.

Jubilee in resplendent colours, when the fruit of hard work is the reason for a celebration in life, what could be more suitable in the decorations than fruit itself?

Birthday party full of atmosphere, red symbolizes love and affection, appropriate for this occasion. In the abundance aof fruit and flowers lie the wishes for happiness and passion.

Feste feiern. Das ist zwar nicht allein dem Herbst vorbehalten. Doch erhalten sie in dieser Jahreszeit eine besonders üppige Ausprägung. Das gesamte Spektrum der Blumenfarben läuft jetzt zu Hochtouren auf. Die Natur läßt ihr Blätterwerk in allen nur erdenklichen Nuancierungen schillern, und die Erntekörbe sind mit dem reichen und farbenprächtigen Früchtesegen prall gefüllt. Da läßt es sich vortrefflich feiern, zumal wenn die Tischdekorationen in jeglicher Hinsicht aus dem Vollen schöpfen. Das Zusammenspiel aller Töne wird zu einem Feuerwerk der Formen und Farben. Doch nicht minder herausfordernd ist es, mit der Beschränkung auf wenige Töne entsprechende Ruhe, Konzentration und würdige Untermalung auszudrücken. Alle Ideen sind mit wenigen Veränderungen in jede Jahreszeit zu übertragen. Wo die herbstlichen Chrysanthemen stehen, können im Frühjahr Tulpen, im Sommer Rosen verwendet werden. Nichts ist statisch. Vielmehr kommt es auf sensibles Gespür an, mit den Blumen den Feieranlass zu umrahmen.

Klassische Hochzeit, eine farblich zurückhaltende Tischdekoration, die den zweiten Blick auf das Grün und allerhand Interessantes herausfordert.

Formvollendete Verlobung, in Violett, aufgehellt mit weißen Blüten sowie Grau- und Silberanteilen, die eine jugendliche und locker wirkende Stimmung entstehen lassen.

Liebliche Taufe, Rosen und allerlei lieblich wirkende Blüten machen unmissverständlich den freudigen Anlass deutlich. Zarte Farbnuancierungen dem Kind zu Ehren.

Farbenprächtiges Jubiläum, wenn die Früchte eines reifen Lebens Anlass für ein Fest sind, dann dürfen solche auch dasselbe dekorativ begleiten.

Stimmungsvoller Geburtstag, Rot symbolisiert Liebe und Zuneigung, passend zu diesem Anlass. In der Glut der Früchte und Blüten liegt der Wunsch auf Glück und Leidenschaft.

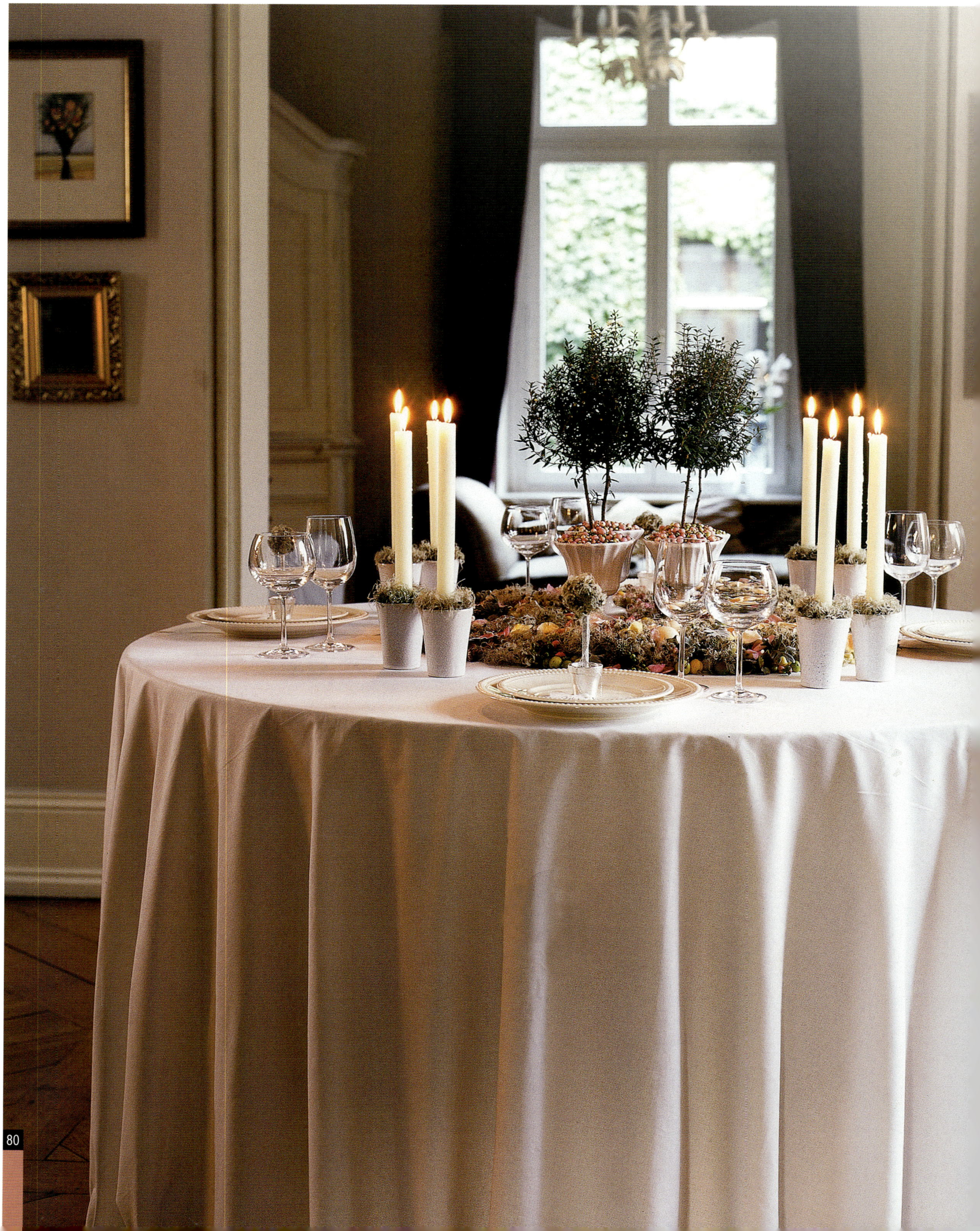

Classic wedding
Klassische Hochzeit

Die klassische Hochzeit modern interpretiert mit Myrte. Eine arabische Legende besagt, dass Adam und Eva bei der Vertreibung aus dem Paradies drei Dinge mitnehmen durften. Adam griff nach Datteln zur Erinnerung an die Süße des Paradieses, Eva nahm Weizenähren, weil sie das beste Mehl ergeben, und gemeinsam griffen sie nach Myrtenzweigen wegen ihres köstlichen Duftes. Noch tausend Jahre später nehmen auswandernde Griechen Myrte als Symbol der Heimat, des paradiesischen Glücks und der Schönheit der Welt mit an ihren neuen Standort. Was wäre also als Grünakzent passender, um einen neuen Lebensabschnitt zu beginnen, als die Myrte? Kaum eine klassische Hochzeit, bei der die Myrte nicht eine Rolle spielte. Man kennt sie zur Girlande gewunden, die das Tor zum Altar ziert, als kleine Sträußchen am Jackett des Bräutigams getragen oder Bestandteil des Brautstraußes.
Sehr zentral wird die Myrte auch bei der runden Tischdekoration zur Hochzeit eingesetzt: als dekorative Myrtenbäumchen, um die herum sich die festlich geschmückten Kerzen und die zartfarbige Blüten- und Fruchtdekoration ranken.

The classic wedding in a modern interpretation with myrtle. According to an Arabian legend, Adam and Eve were allowed to take three things with them when they left the garden of Paradise. Adam wanted dates, as they would always remind him of the sweetness of Paradise. Eve chose ears of wheat because they make the best flour, and together they decided on myrtle branches for their delicious scent. Even a thousand years later, emigrating Greeks took myrtle branches with them as a symbol of their homeland, and of idyllic happiness and the beauty of the world.
So what could be a more appropriate green highlight for beginning a new life phase than myrtle? Hardly a classic wedding takes place without myrtle playing a role. Familiar to most of us, either wound into a garland for decorating the archway to the altar, as a boutonnière on the lapel of the groom, or a component of the bridal bouquet. Therefore myrtle is also included in this round wedding table decoration: as mini-myrtle trees set in the centre of an arrangement of winding vines, delicately pastel flowers and fruit, and escorted by festively decorated candles.

Gefässe (Veip), Kerzen (AV), Geschirr, Gläser (Becker), handgeschöpftes Papier (Pulsar)

plant holders (Veip), candles (AV), dishes, glasses (Becker), handmade paper (Pulsar)

Klassische Hochzeit. Eine Tischdekoration, die sehr edel aussieht und doch eine relativ preiswerte Lösung darstellt. Die Myrtenbäumchen werden in passende Gefäße gesetzt und die Erde mit den rosigen Früchten der Schneebeere abgedeckt. Sie können bereits Tage vor der Hochzeit vorbereitet werden und werden noch Wochen und Monate später als Fensterschmuck an diesen Tag erinnern. Die Blütenfläche in der Mitte auf der Hochzeitstafel besteht aus einem passend zugeschnittenen Maschendrahtgeflecht, in das die flauschigen Fruchtstände der *Clematis* eingewoben sind. Allerlei Blütenblätter in zarten Pastellfarben und Früchte bringen die farbliche Entsprechung. Die platzanweisenden Tischkarten der Gäste sind Nachbildungen der Myrtenbäumchen, eine mit Sprühkleber geformte Kugel aus Myrtenzweigen und *Clematis*-Früchten, die mit einem Holzstab versehen in einem Tontopf steht.
Die komplette Versilberung unterstreicht den Festanlass. Töpfe bilden auch die Kerzenhalterung, eine einfach zu bewerkstelligende Anregung.

Classic wedding. A table decoration which looks very aristocratic, but which can be created relatively inexpensively. The myrtle trees are set in matching white pots, the earth covered with snowberries, the rosy fruit of *Symphoricarpos albus*. These can be prepared days before the wedding, and even weeks and months later they will still make pretty windowsill decorations to remember the big day.
The floral arrangement in the centre of the wedding table is based on a piece of mesh wire, cut to size and interwoven with feathery *Clematis* inflorescence. Fruit and all kinds of flower petals in delicate pastel shades provide the colour highlights. The name cards for the guests are miniature copies of the myrtle trees, made of myrtle twigs and *Clematis* rolled into little balls and affixed with spray glue, then attached to small wooden sticks inserted in clay pots. The overall coating of shiny silver underscores the festive atmosphere of the day. Tiny plant pots are also used for the candle holders, an easy-to-make inspiration.

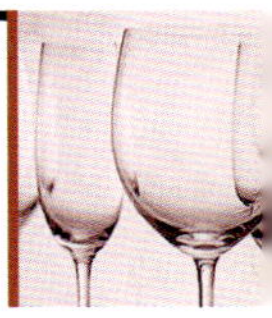

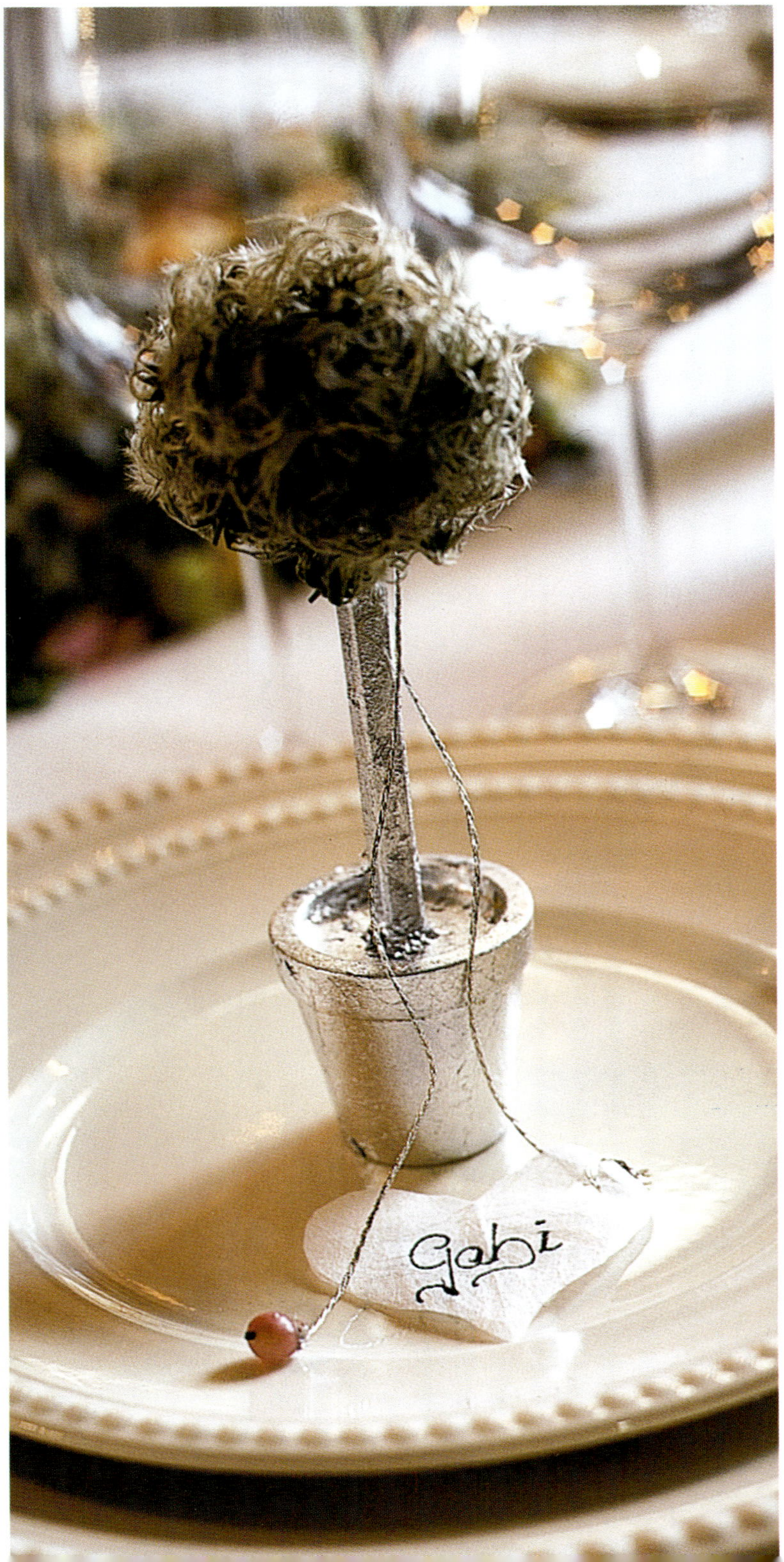
Gabi

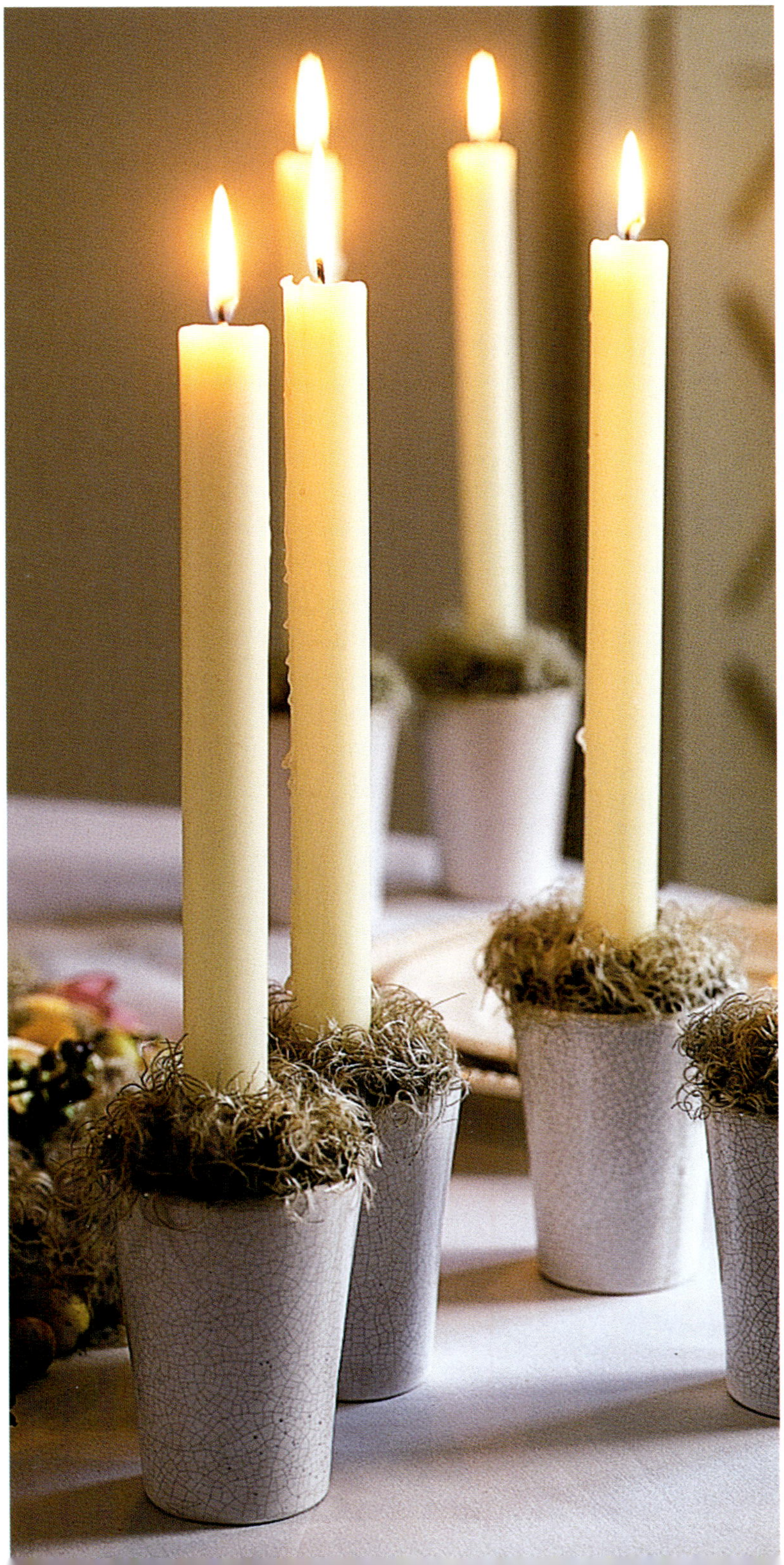

Klassische Hochzeit. Eine klassisch-edle Ausstrahlung wird auch immer mit einem Orchideenblütenschmuck erreicht. Wem die kugeligen Myrtenbäumchen zu wenig blumig sind, kann bereits mit drei blühenden Orchideenpflanzen eine alternative Tischdekoration erzielen. Unter den ausschwingenden Rispen der *Phalaenopsis* getafelt zu haben, wird keinesfalls den Gedanken an eine preisgünstige Tischdekoration aufkommen lassen, die diese im Vergleich zu den sonst üblichen und aufwendigen Blumengestecken ist.

Weil alles Weitere den schmetterlingsähnlichen Blüten den Rang ablaufen würde, ist die runde Tischplatte schlicht mit Blütenblätter von Chrysanthemen ausgestreut. Hierauf kommen die gläsernen, rauchigen Vasen, die die ausgewaschenen Wurzeln der Orchideenpflanzen erkennen lassen. Wie die Partner einer Ehe in ihrer Unterschiedlichkeit einer den anderen ergänzt, so gehen auch hier die Glasvasen mit dem transparenten Geschirr eine harmonische und wie selbstverständlich wirkende Verbindung ein.

Classic wedding. A classic and aristocratic atmosphere can also be achieved with a decoration of orchid flowers. For those who find the myrtle trees lacking in flowers, an arrangement with as little as three orchids can make a lovely table decoration. No one who has dined under the swaying panicles of *Phalaenopsis* will ever think that the table decoration was cheaply made – which this one is, compared to the usual complicated and time-consuming bouquets. As anything more would take the limelight away from the butterfly-like blossoms, the surface of the table is simply strewn with *Chrysanthemum* petals.
Set on this fragrant tablecloth, the smoky glass vases – whose clarity allows the rinsed roots of the orchid plants to add to the classic creation – pair up harmoniously with the matching glass dishes.

Vasen (Broste Design), Glasteller (Kehrle), Gläser (Becker)

vases (Broste Design), glass plates (Kehrle), glasses (Becker)

Besonders im Herbst lässt sich aus der Fülle der Blumen reichhaltig schöpfen.
Und selbst bei einer farblichen Reduzierung auf Blau, Violett, Lila bis Rosé bietet diese Jahreszeit Vielfalt. Abgestimmt auf die Blütenmenge, und gleichzeitig den klassischen Stil unterstreichend, ziehen Füllhörner aus Schleierkraut gewickelt das Augenmerk auf sich. Aufstrebend auf schlankem Stab und scheinbar über den kastigen Gefäßen schwebend, geben sie der Festtafel anlässlich einer Verlobungsfeier eine beschwingt-fröhliche wie liebevolle Unterstreichung. Dieser blütenreiche und formvollendete Schmuck passt sogar in ein eher friesisch-ländliches Ambiente mit blau-weiß gestrichenen Türen und Fensterrahmen. Natürlich darf die Rose nicht fehlen. Als Symbol der jungen Liebe fügt sie sich in ihren pastelligen Tönen harmonisch ein.

Engagement party in perfect form

Formvollendete Verlobung

Particularly in autumn the abundance of flowers and plants is a "horn of plenty". And even when the colours are restricted to blue, violet, lilac and rosé, this season offers a diversity like no other. With a carefully-calculated amount of flowers and underscoring the classic style, this elegant horn of plenty with its trailing Gypsophila is a real eye-catcher. Posing like gymnasts on thin poles and appearing to float over their boxy pedestals, they give the festive table for the engagement party a light-hearted and loving atmosphere. With its many flowers and perfect form, this decoration even fits in well in the countrified Friesian style house with its the blue-and-white doors and window-sills. Naturally there must also be roses present. As a symbol of young love, they blend in harmoniously with their delicate pastel shades.

Gefäße, Herzen (Kayak), Kordel (Halbach), Geschirr, Gläser (Becker), Perlmuttaccessoires (Des Pots)

pots, hearts (Kayak), cord (Halbach), dishes, glasses (Becker), mother-of-pearl accessories (Des Pots)

Formvollendete Verlobung. Auch bei den Tischkarten wird die Form des Füllhorns aufgegriffen. Schlanker und zarter als beim eigentlichen Blütenschmuck, aber mit der gleichen Assoziation an die Klassik. Diese Hörnchen sind aus „Angelhair", einem metallischen Gespinst, geformt, mit einer dutenden Einzelrose gefüllt und dem Namensschild versehen. Ihre großen Vorbilder dagegen brauchen zur Stabilität, um die Menge an Blumen und der wasserhaltenden Blumensteckmasse aufnehmen zu können, ein Maschendrahtgerüst. Folie kleidet sie von innen aus, damit kein Wasser auf die Tischdecke tropft. Für den sicheren Stand ist der Stab im Gefäß einbetoniert.

So kann nichts umfallen. Passend dazu das Tischaccessoire in Form eines Betonherzens. Symbol, guter Wunsch und dekoratives Element für die Verlobungsfeier des jungen Paares gleichermaßen.

Engagement party in perfect form. The name card holders also reflect the shape of the horn of plenty. Slimmer and more delicate than their larger cousins, but with the same association to the classic form. These tiny horns are made of angel hair – a tangled mass of metal wires – and contain a single, sweet-smelling rose in their open end with the name tag attached to the tip. A supporting frame of mesh wire gives the larger creations additional stability to hold aloft the masses of flowers and floral foam full of water. Inside they have a plastic lining to prevent water from dripping onto the tablecloth. For further support, the end of the pole is embedded in cement, to make sure that nothing can tip over.

The cement heart on the table is a symbol of good luck as well as a fitting decorative element for the engagement of the young couple.

Betongefäße, Drahtformelemente (Kayak), Glasgefäße (Tel), Kerzen (Arte), Kräuter (Pinaruh)

cement pots, wire form elements (Kayak), glasses (Tel), candles (Arte), herbs (Pinaruh)

Formvollendete Verlobung.
Aufgedreht im wahrsten Sinne des Wortes. Auch so wird eine alte Formensprache modern interpretiert und passt sich damit zeitgemäßen Räumen an.

Die runden Drahtkugeln erinnern an beschnittene Buchsbaum-Bäumchen, die im Barock en vogue waren. Sie sind mit allerlei Krautigem gefüllt, was dem festlichen Anlass nicht nur eine duftige Note verleiht, sondern auch noch schnell zu erstellen ist. Denn nichts muss drappiert, geformt oder akkurat gestaltet werden. Ein loses Miteinander von Duftblättern, Blüten und Zweigen bringt die richtige Wirkung.

Die Befestigung der Drahtbäume in den Gefäßen erfolgt genauso standfest wie bei den Füllhörnern zuvor: mit Beton. Und wem Floralgestaltungen für einen einzigen schönen Tag zu aufwendig erscheinen, dem sei versichert, dass solcherlei Drahtbäume jederzeit wieder einsatzfähig sind, dann vielleicht mit Blütenbändern umwunden, von Schleierkraut umkränzt oder von Efeu erklommen.

Engagement party in perfect form.
High spirits in every sense of the word. A new interpretation of an old form which suits its contemporary settings. The round wiry spheres are reminiscent of the well-groomed box trees that were in style in the Baroque period. They are filled with an assortment of greens and herbs, which not only add a fragrant note to the celebration, but are also easily and quickly made. Because their contents are neither accurately draped, formed or structured, but rather just a loose jumble of fragrant leaves, flowers and twigs. The "trunks" of the trees are as securely "rooted" as the poles supporting the horns of plenty: they are "planted" in cement. And those who find this too much work for just one day's festivities can rest assured that such wired creations can be used again and again, either wound about with flowers chains, rings of *Gypsophila* or wreaths of ivy.

91

Glasgefäße (Sandra Rich), Geschirr (Broste Design), Tischwäsche (ASA), Servietten (Lazis), Kristallschmuck (Des Pots), handgeschöpftes Papier (Pulsar), Keramikgefäße (Ronkenstein), Band (Vaban)

glasses (Sandra Rich), dishes (Broste Design), table liner (ASA), serviettes (Lazis), crystal pendants (Des Pots), handmade paper (Pulsar), ceramic pots (Ronkenstein), ribbon (Vaban)

Sweet and charming baptism
Liebliche Taufe

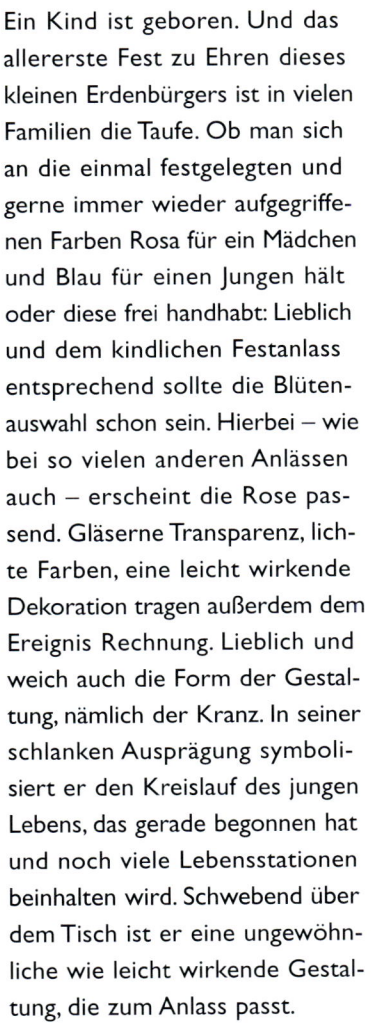

Ein Kind ist geboren. Und das allererste Fest zu Ehren dieses kleinen Erdenbürgers ist in vielen Familien die Taufe. Ob man sich an die einmal festgelegten und gerne immer wieder aufgegriffenen Farben Rosa für ein Mädchen und Blau für einen Jungen hält oder diese frei handhabt: Lieblich und dem kindlichen Festanlass entsprechend sollte die Blütenauswahl schon sein. Hierbei – wie bei so vielen anderen Anlässen auch – erscheint die Rose passend. Gläserne Transparenz, lichte Farben, eine leicht wirkende Dekoration tragen außerdem dem Ereignis Rechnung. Lieblich und weich auch die Form der Gestaltung, nämlich der Kranz. In seiner schlanken Ausprägung symbolisiert er den Kreislauf des jungen Lebens, das gerade begonnen hat und noch viele Lebensstationen beinhalten wird. Schwebend über dem Tisch ist er eine ungewöhnliche wie leicht wirkende Gestaltung, die zum Anlass passt.

A child is born. And the very first occasion to honour the arrival of this small citizen for many families is the baptism ceremony. Whether one decides to go with the traditional – and still beloved – colour code of pink for a girl and blue for a boy or to ignore such restrictions, the choice of flowers should still be in sweet charming shades appropriate for babies.

As on so many important occasions the rose also seems suitable here. The transparency of glass, the pale colours and light and airy decorations are also just right for the event. Even the shape of the creation – a wreath – is baby-sweet and soft. With its stylishly slim lines it symbolizes the cycle of the life which has just begun and which has yet to pass by many stations on the road of life. Floating serenely over the table, the wreath is an unusual and light-as-a-feather creation which is wonderfully appropriate for the occasion.

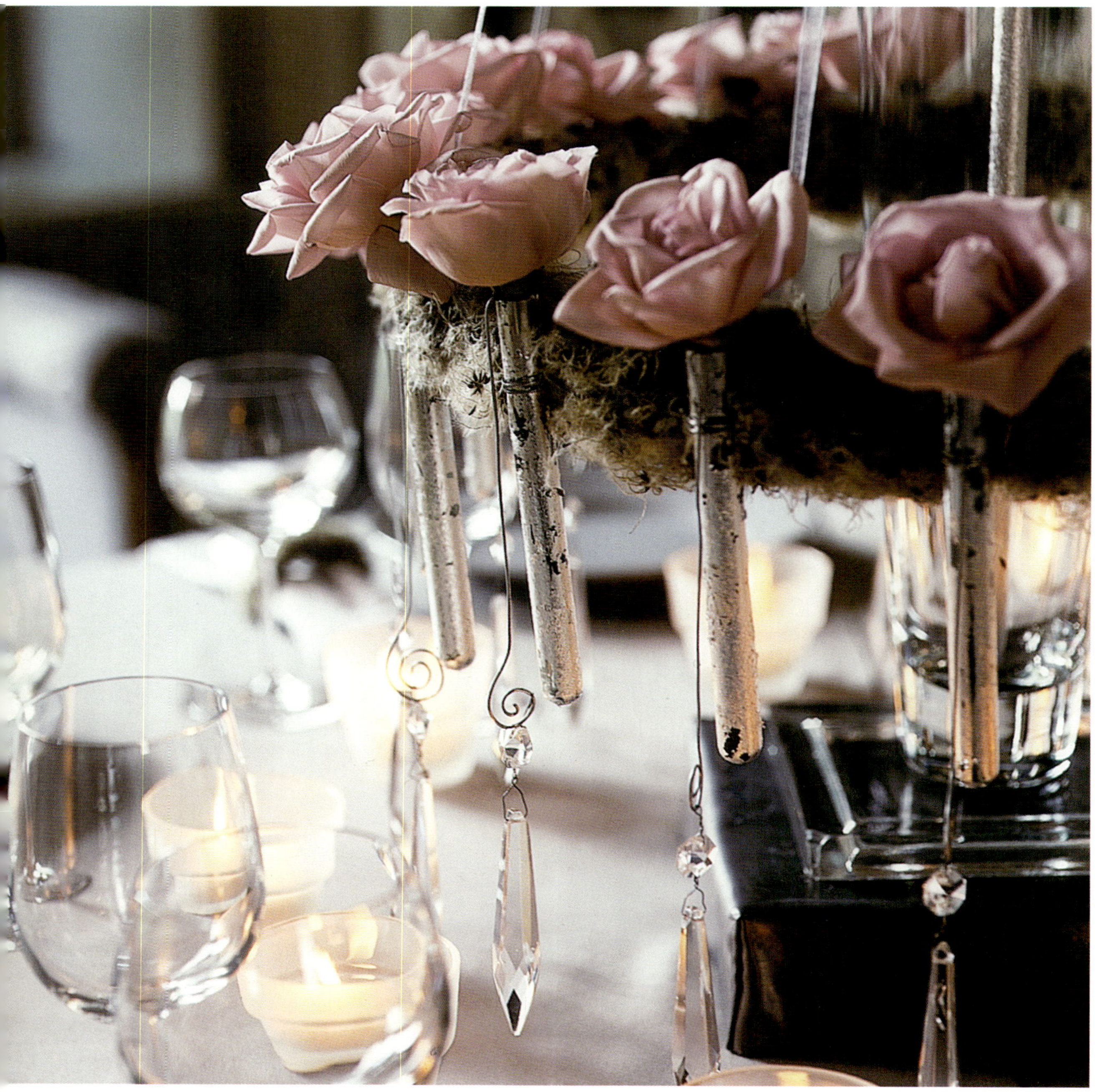

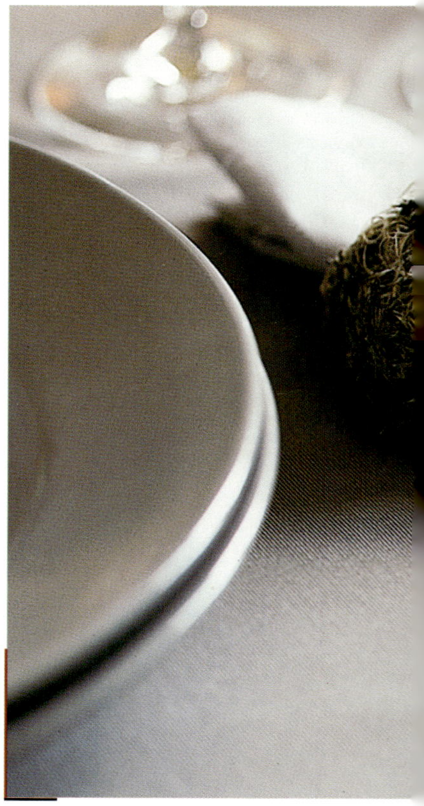

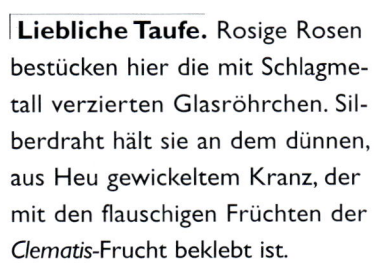

Liebliche Taufe. Rosige Rosen bestücken hier die mit Schlagmetall verzierten Glasröhrchen. Silberdraht hält sie an dem dünnen, aus Heu gewickeltem Kranz, der mit den flauschigen Früchten der *Clematis*-Frucht beklebt ist.
Zur Auflockerung und spielerischen Akzentuierung ist Kristallschmuck an zur Schnecke geformtem Spanndraht gehängt, das Statisch-Formale dezent auflockernd.
Auch bei den Tischkarten findet sich die selbstgebogene Schneckenform mit dem Schmuckelement wieder. Der Kranz selbst hängt wie an einem Maibaum oder Richtfestschmuck an einem langen Stab, der aufrecht in einer überaus schlanken, hohen Glasvase geführt wird. Um dieser Glasvase mehr Präsenz zu verleihen, steht sie auf einem mit Walzblei verkleideten Podest in der Tischmitte.
Der Serviettenring greift die Oberflächenbeschaffenheit des Kranzes auf, indem auch er mit *Clematis* beklebt und zusätzlich mit Drahtschnecke und Kristallanhänger verziert ist.

|Sweet and charming baptism. Pink roses adorn the glass tubes in their silver-plated "booties". Silver wires affix them to the thin wreath of intertwined hay, which is stuck all over with fluffy *Clematis* inflorescence. To loosen up the otherwise static and formal arrangement and to provide playful accents, crystal pendants are hung from the wreath on wires bent into the shape of snails. This motif is found again in the name card holders. The wreath itself hangs on a long pole, similar to the decorations for a maypole or roofing ceremony. This pole is anchored in a tall glass vase, which is given increased presence by its pedestal covered in rolled metal and positioned in the centre of the table. The serviette ring repeats the soft gentle contours of the wreath as it is also covered with *Clematis*, and each serviette also sports its own snail-shaped wire and crystal pendant.

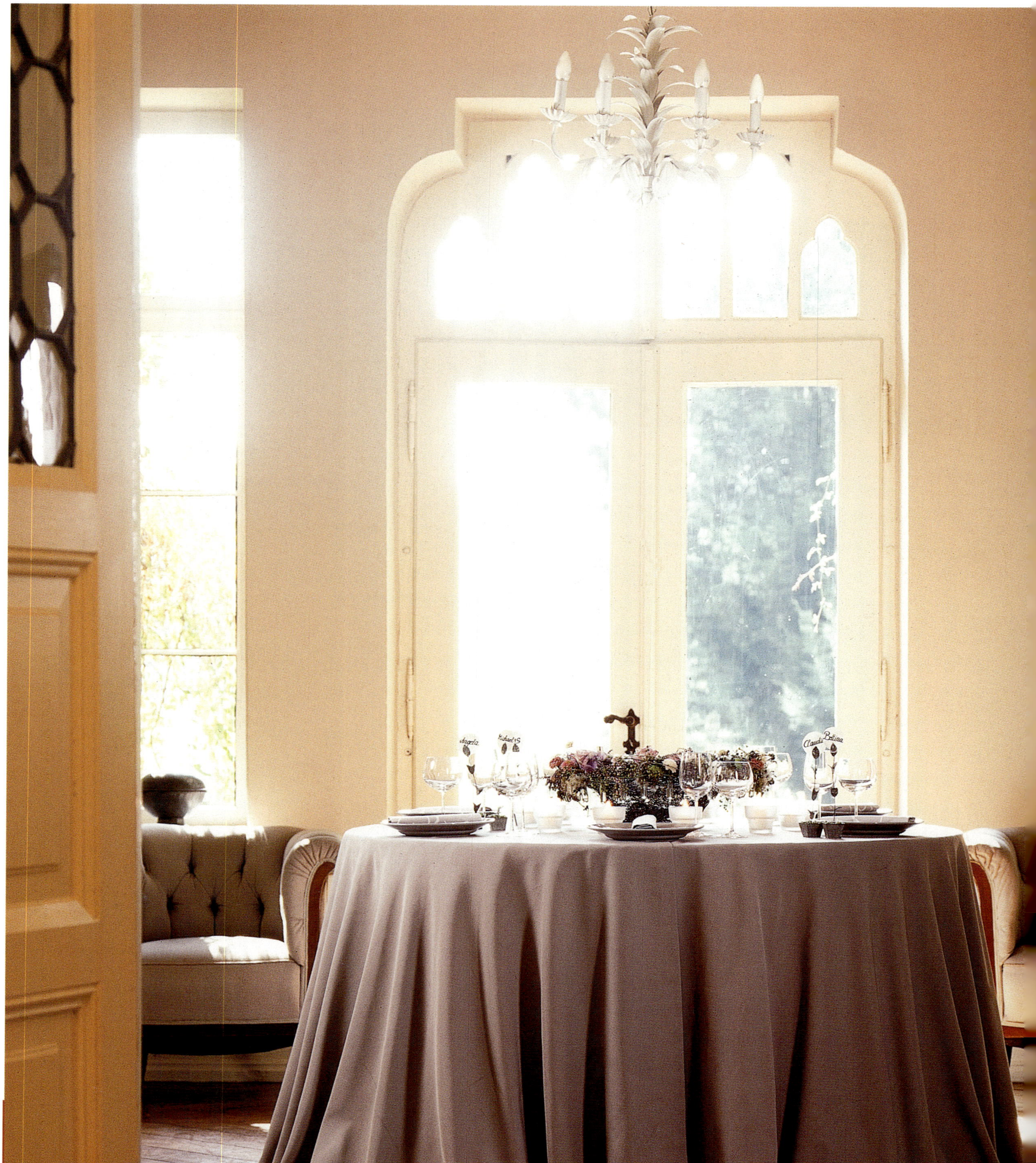

Geschirr, Namensschilder (Broste Design), Servietten (Lazis), Wickeldraht (Braucke), Gläser (Becker), Kerzen (AV), Glasröhrchen (Floristenbedarf)

dishes, name tags (Broste Design), serviettes (Lazis), spooled wire (Braucke), glasses (Becker), candles (AV), glass tubes (florist supply)

Sweet and charming baptism. The wreath as a symbol at a baptism celebration can also be placed horizontally in the centre of the table. This draws the eyes of every guest seated at the table, especially if it is slightly raised on a delicate and tasteful pedestal, on which it appears to float over the table.

Because the wreath itself is not a single element, but rather the decorative edge of a handmade basket of interwoven wires. In this are set the glass tubes for holding the flowers. In addition to the flowers in the arrangement – which can be changed any time – fruit and other decorative accessories can fill the inside of the basket.

Add to this the metal name cards for the godparents and other guests, made in the shape of stems and leaves, and the table is complete.

Liebliche Taufe. Der Kranz als Symbol bei der Feier anlässlich einer Taufe kann aber auch in der liegenden Form den mittig platzierten Tischschmuck bilden. Alle Blikke der daran Sitzenden werden sich auf ihn konzentrieren, wenn er wie leicht erhöht auf einem zarten und unauffällig wirkenden Gestell scheinbar zu schweben scheint. Denn der Kranz selbst ist nicht etwa ein eigenes Element. Vielmehr bildet er den Rand des selbsterstellten Korbes, der aus abgespultem und zu einer Korbform gebogenem Drahtgeflecht besteht.

Dieser wird mit Glasröhrchen versehen, die die Blüten aufnehmen. Zusätzlich zu diesem blumigen und jederzeit auswechselbaren Blumenschmuck können Früchte und andere dekorative Accessoires das tiefliegende Innere des Korbes ausfüllen. Alternativ hierzu dann die Namensschildchen der Paten und Taufgäste aus Metall in Stängel- und Blattform.

metal cups (Des Pots), candles (AV), artichokes, eucalyptus bark, fruit (Pinaruh), cord (Halbach)

Metallbecher (Des Pots), Kerzen (AV), Artischocken, Eucalyptusrinde, Früchte (Pinaruh), Kordel (Halbach)

Jubilee in resplendent colours
Farbenprächtiges Jubiläum

Das Jubiläum. Ein bestimmter Lebensabschnitt privater oder beruflicherseits ist erreicht. Meist nach einer Reihe an bestimmten Jahren, 10, 20 oder 25, die nun im offiziellen oder halboffiziellen Rahmen gefeiert werden. Reden werden gehalten, die die Verdienste dieses Menschen darstellen. Im übertragenen Sinne sind es die Früchte dieses Lebens, die bei der Jubiläumsfeier im Mittelpunkt stehen, die vor Jahren gesät, nun zum Erfolg oder besonderen Verdienst gereift den Geladenen dargeboten werden. Insofern liegt der Gedanke sehr nahe, bei der Tischdekoration für diesen Anlass tatsächlich viele Früchte einzusetzen, die gerade die herbstliche Natur in ihrer gesamten Farbenpracht und Vielfalt bereithält. Sie werden einfach in die Mitte der langen Tafel gleichmäßig verteilt, wie ein langes Band, den Fluß des Lebens symbolisierend. Und von Kerzen, in Artischocken gesteckt, oder auch Teelichtern begleitet. Von solch einer Tischdekoration darf sogar genascht werden. Je nach Belieben kann diese Dekoration auch durch herbstliche Blüten oder Blättern begleitet werden. Zu den Ähren können sich Sonnenblumenblüten gesellen, die auch ohne Wasserversorgung eine gute Haltbarkeit aufweisen. Und wenn es sich um ein „goldenes" Jubiläum handelt, könnten einzelne Früchte mit Blatt überzogen hinzugefügt werden.

A jubilee or anniversary. A very special phase of life has been completed – if personal or professional. Usually after a certain number of years – 10, 20 or 25 – which is now to be celebrated, however formally. Speeches are made in which the achievements of the guest of honour are described. Figuratively speaking, it is the fruits of labour in life that are the focus of such celebrations. Fruit from seeds sown long ago, now ripened into success or some special achievement, and held up to the guests on this special occasion. Therefore it is only logical that the fitting decoration for such an occasion would be fruit, which nature in autumn offers in great resplendence and diversity. Simply arranged in even distribution along the centre of the long table in a long flowing line, symbolizing the river of life. Accompanied by candles placed in holders made of artichokes. And the best aspect of such table decorations is that they are also edible.

Depending on personal taste, the decoration can also be supplemented by autumn blooms or leaves. The wheat can be paired up with sunflowers, which keep well for a time without an additional water supply. And if the occasion is also a "golden" anniversary, individual fruits overlaid with gold plate can be added to the arrangement.

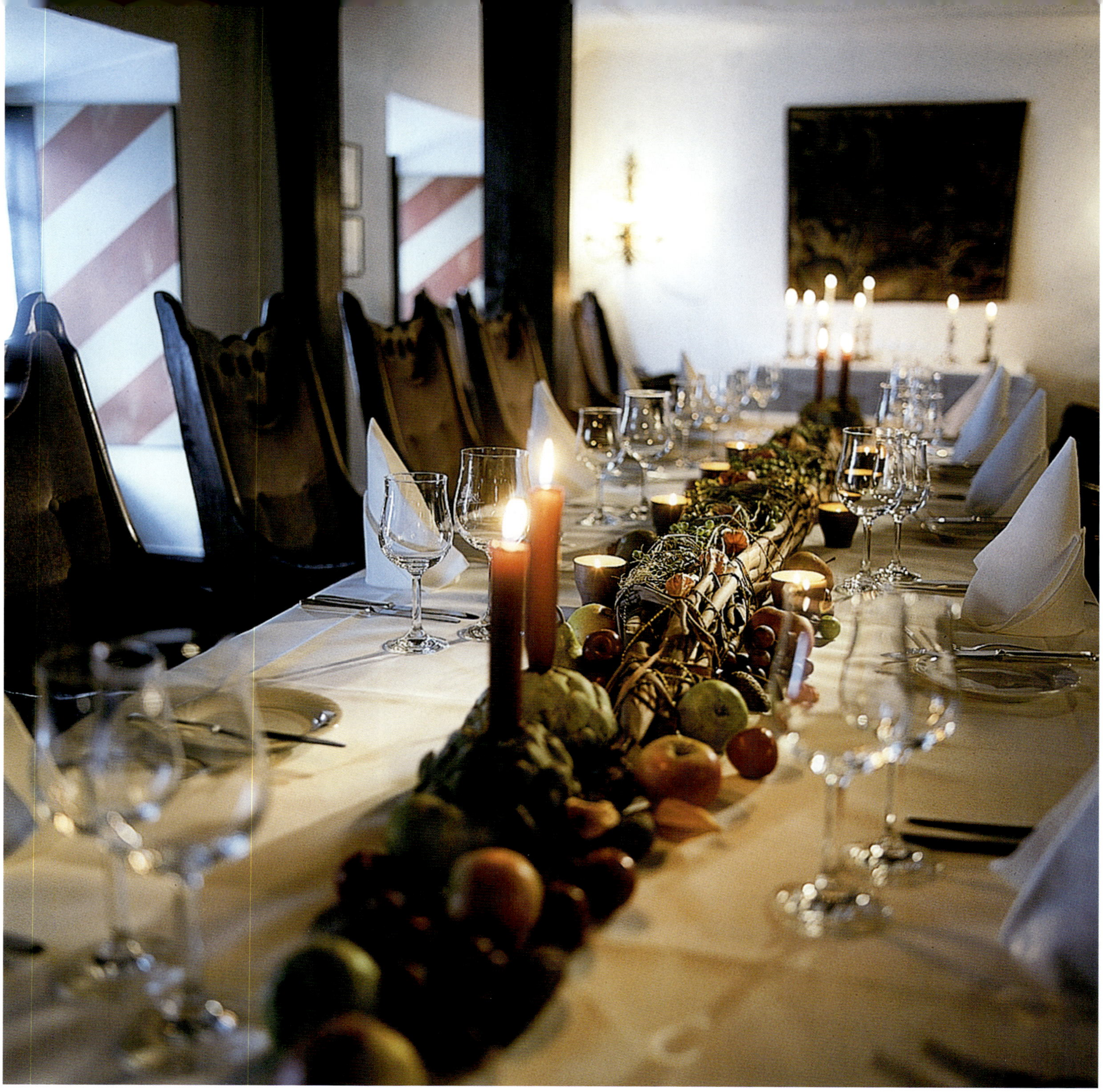

Farbenprächtiges Jubiläum. Um dem mittig platzierten Früchteband eine Struktur und Plastizität zu geben, ist ein rinnenartiges Grundgerüst aus Maschendraht gefertigt und mit *Eucalyptus*-Rinde bewickelt worden. Damit diese für das Bewickeln nicht zu sperrig ist, kann sie zuvor ein paar Stunden in Wasser eingeweicht werden. Eine goldene Kordel ist zusätzlicher Halt und Zierde gleichermaßen. Für die Kerzenhalterung aus Artischocken sind diese an der Spitze gekappt und mit einem Loch zur Aufnahme der Stabkerze versehen worden. Kleine Mini-Artischocken bilden passend dazu den Serviettenschmuck, der von den Gästen als Erinnerung mit nach Hause genommen werden soll. Der Artischokenstängel ist mit Blattgold akzentuiert. Wer kein Blattgold zur Hand hat, kann den Stängel auch mit einer goldenen Kordel mehrmals dekorativ bewickeln.

Jubilee in resplendent colours. To give the river of fruit in the centre of the table additional stability, a trough-like structure of mesh wire is formed and interwoven with strips of eucalyptus bark. So that these rinds are not too bulky to work with, they can be soaked for a few hours in water beforehand. A golden cord gives additional support and also adornment. To make the artichoke candleholders, the tip is cut off and a hole hollowed out to the exact size of the candle. Miniature artichokes make matching serviette accessories, which the guests can take home as souvenirs. The stem of the artichoke is accentuated with gold plate. If gold plate is not available, the stem can also be wound about with decorative gold cord.

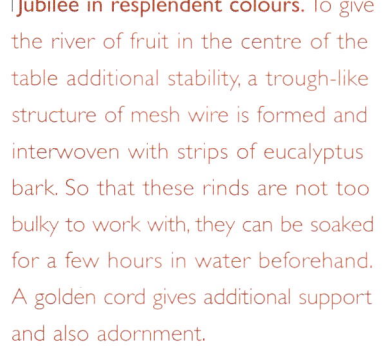

Farbenprächtiges Jubiläum. Eine schnell zu erstellende wie unkonventionell wirkende Tafeldekoration. Statt der reinen Fruchtgirlande über die Länge der Tafel kann auch ein Band aus einem Töpfchenallerlei gestaltet werden. Als verbindende Gestaltung dient ein langes, schmales Fries aus den Früchten des Perückenstrauches. Dazu werden die flauschigen Fruchtstände zwischen Zeitungspapier gelegt und bei mittlerer Hitze gebügelt. So verbinden sie sich filzartig miteinander und dienen als natürliche Sets. Die Töpfe sind mit Frischsteckmasse gefüllt und jeweils einer einzelnen Blumenart Kopf-an-Kopf besteckt.

Andere blattvergoldete Töpfchen nehmen die Stumpenkerzen auf oder dienen einzelnen, farbenprächtigen Früchten als Präsentationsfläche. Ein paar Blütenblätter dazwischen gestreut, geben dem Tischschmuck weitere Farbtupfer. Die zur Tüte gerollte und mit einem Metallblatt gehaltene Serviette nimmt ebenfalls Früchte auf. Trotz der unkomplizierten Machart dieser Gestaltung, entbehrt sie nicht an herbstlicher Prächtigkeit, saisonaler Opulenz und anlassgemässer Gediegenheit.

Jubilee in resplendent colours. An unconventional yet easy-to-make table decoration. Instead of the fruit garland down the length of the table, a procession of various different pots can be assembled. The connecting element is a long narrow mat of *Cotinus* inflorescence. To make this, the fluffy fibres are laid between newspapers and flattened with a moderately warm iron. The heat causes them to stick together to form a natural mat.

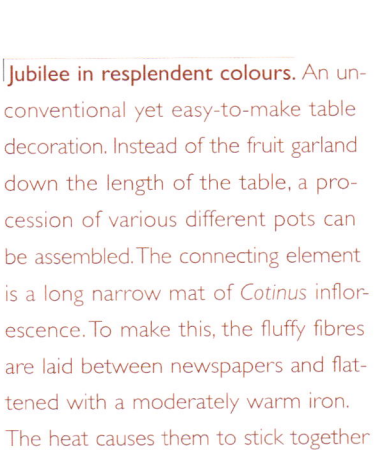

The pots are filled with floral foam and each pot is then decorated with its own single kind of flower, arranged face-to-face. Other gold-plated pots become candleholders or serve as presentation platters for individual dramatically-coloured fruits. A few flower petals strewn on the table give the table decoration an additional colour highlight.

The serviette, rolled into a cone and held by the coiled stem of a metal leaf, also carries its portion of fruit. Despite the uncomplicated construction of this creation, it is not at all lacking in autumn magnificence, opulence and distinction in keeping with the occasion.

Gefäße (Des Pots), Metallblatt (Kayak), Gimpe (Halbach)

pots (Des Pots), metal leaf (Kayak), gimp (Halbach)

Glasgefäße (Veip), Glasbecher (Haymann), Kerzen (Arte), Stühle (Lazis), Glasgeschirr (Becker)

glass vases (Veip), glasses (Haymann), candles (Arte), chairs (Lazis), glass dishes (Becker)

Birthday party full of atmosphere
Stimmungsvoller Geburtstag

In vielen Ländern ist es üblich, dass Freunde und Familienangehörige die Feier für das Geburtstagskind ausrichten. Eigentlich ein schöner Brauch, denn so kann derjenige, der an diesem Tag im Mittelpunkt stehen soll, sich ganz auf das Fest und seine Gäste konzentrieren, während nach mitteleuropäischem Gepflogenheit von ihm die Gastgeberrolle nach allen Regeln der Kunst erwartet wird. Egal, ob nun das Fest für denjenigen, der Geburtstag hat, ausgerichtet wird oder dieser selbst Hand anlegen muss, ein stimmungsvoller Tischschmuck ganz in der roten Vielfalt herbstlichen Beerenallerleis gehalten, wird nachhaltigen Eindruck hinterlassen. Dazu rote Kerzen und vielleicht ein Menü, das ebenfalls in starkem Masse die Farbe Rot aufgreift, und Beerenbowle. Das schwarze Tischtuch ist sicherlich ungewöhnlich, verstärkt aber die sehr sinnliche Ausstrahlung dieser Dekorations-Idee.

In many countries it is the custom for family and friends to give the party for a person celebrating their birthday – often as a surprise. Actually a nice tradition because that way the birthday girl or boy can concentrate fully on enjoying the festivities and devote themselves to their guests. In central Europe, on the contrary, everyone is expected to assume the role of host or hostess on their birthday. But regardless of who plans the party, jolly table decorations in the entire red spectrum of fall berries and fruit will leave a lasting impression. Add to that red candles and perhaps a menu with dishes reflecting the colour red, and fruit punch. The black tablecloth is certainly unusual, and reinforces the sensual ambience of this decoration concept.

Stimmungsvoller Geburtstag. Ein Spaziergang durch die herbstliche Natur ist der Zusammenstellung dieser Tischdekoration vorangegangen. Hierbei wurden allerlei beerentragende Zweige gesammelt. Vor allem Heckenrosen, Rot- und Weißdorn, Schneeball oder die rosa- bis lilafarbene Schneebeere liefern Reichhaltiges.
Die Zweige werden kurzgeschnitten in hochstielige Gläser gestellt, was trotz der sinnlich-schweren Farbigkeit von Beerenschmuck und schwarzer Tischbedeckung filigrane Leichtigkeit bringt. Im Kerzenlicht spiegelt sich der Beerencocktail in den Gläsern besonders schön wider. Wer keine Beerenbowle anbieten will, dennoch auf diesen Effekt nicht verzichten möchte, kann Karaffen oder Gläser mit farbigem Wasser und einigen Früchten füllen. Das ist eine romantisch-sinnliche Stimmung, bei der man gerne bis in die Nacht hinein weiterfeiern möchte.

Birthday party full of atmosphere. The effect of this table decoration is like a luxurious stroll outdoors in autumn. All kinds of branches and twigs have been collected for it; in particular dog-rose, hawthorn and snowballs, or pink and lilac snowberries add to the ensemble. The branches are cut to short lengths and arranged in glass vases which, despite the opulence of the berries and the black tablecloth, create an atmosphere of lacy airiness.

In the candlelight, the fruit cocktail is reflected romantically in the glasses. For those who are not offering their guests punch but who still want this effect, carafes or glasses can be filled with coloured water and fruit arranged artfully in these. This creates a romantic and sensual atmosphere, which will encourage the party to go on late into the night.

Trinkgläser (Veip), Glasgefäße (Ronkenstein), Kerzen (AV)

drinking glasses (Veip), glasses (Ronkenstein), candles (AV)

Stimmungsvoller Geburtstag. Mit Beeren, besonders die im Herbst reichlich vorhandenen und in sich sehr festen Hagebutten, können Gefäßen eine neue und interessante Oberfläche geben. Die Hagebutten können mit Heißkleber aufgebracht werden. Diese Gestaltungsidee gibt vor allem ausrangierten Gefäßen eine neue Bestimmung, sofern sie von ihrer Materialbeschaffenheit, wasserfest, und Form her als geeignet erscheinen. Diese Vasenoberfläche hält auch über den Feieranlaß hinaus und kann später mit anderen Blüten kombiniert werden. Auch in der anschließenden Advents- und Weihnachtszeit lassen sich die so im Herbst erstellten Gefäße integrieren. Mit etwas Goldspray übersprühen, etwas glänzendes „Engelshaar" aufbringen oder mit Sternenschmuck füllen. Schon ist aus der Geburtstagsdekoration ein weiterer Festschmuck entstanden.

Birthday party full of atmosphere. With berries and fruit, for example rose hips, which are firm and robust and particularly abundant in autumn, pots and vases can be given a new and interesting surface relief. Together with the flowers this makes a fascinating decoration. The berries can be affixed with hot glue. This creative idea is especially useful to give old vases a new lease on life, as long as their shape, material and water-holding properties are suitable. This new party dress for a vase will keep fresh until the festivities are over, and can also be combined later with other flower arrangements. Even in the coming Advent and Christmas season, vases decorated for autumn celebrations can be integrated. Simply cover them with gold spray, add some shiny angel hair or fill them with star-shaped accessories, and already the birthday decorations are ready to join in other festivities again.

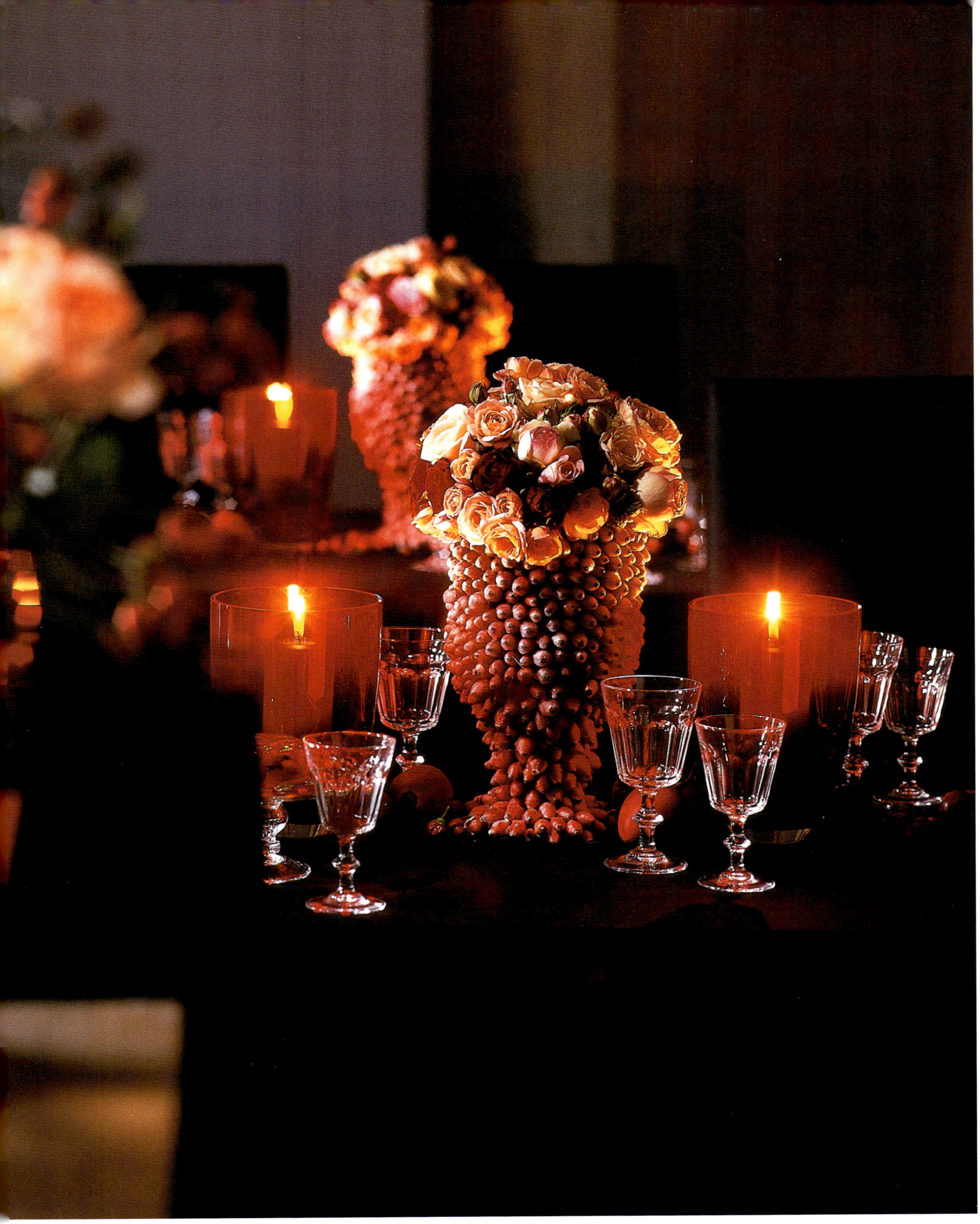

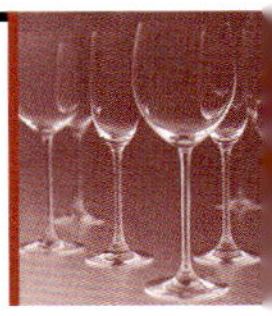

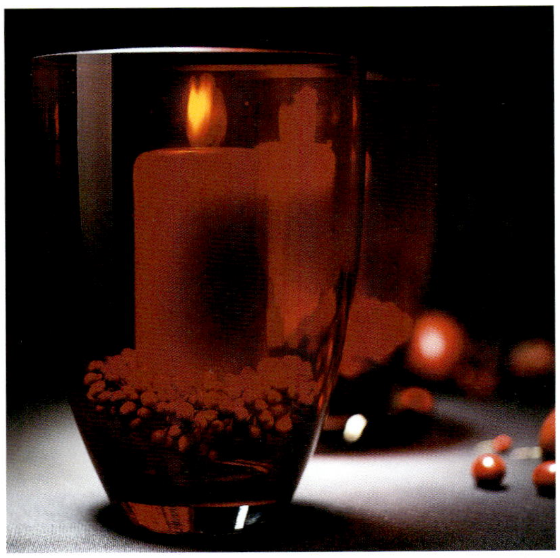

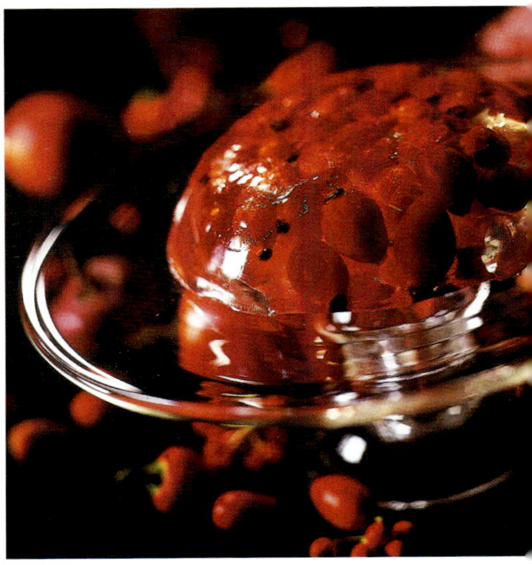

110

WinterRendezvous

WinterRendezvous

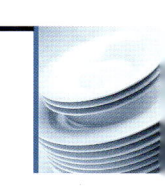

Frost flowers could be symbolic of the last and coldest season of the year. But at the same time, they can create a warm-hearted, emotional and sensual ambience in table decorations. If not so many flowers are available, perhaps natural materials and fibres in combination with accessories can be brought to the fore. Their textures, structures and material properties can make an attractive and decorative picture when combined in an imaginative way with the attributes typical of wintertime. The luminosity of summer and the diversity of shapes and colours in autumn are compensated in winter by candlelight. Its warm glow bathes the lovingly decorated table in an atmosphere that captures the heart.
Table in magnificent purple, dark warm red shades are in style all year round. Although toned down a bit in combination with elegant grey in winter, it still underscores the festive magnificence.
Invitation to Advent tea, the colours and perfume of beeswax, cinnamon, liquorice and cloves combine to make a table decoration full of atmosphere which will help your guests forget the cold of winter.
Christmas rendezvous, memories of childhood Christmases come alive again. But the traditional red and green duo is given a new and contemporary interpretation here.
Star-studded table art, black and white, colours which draw attention to the basic elements. A table decoration which conveys the meaning of the Christmas celebration with peace and clarity.
Happy New Year, a turn of the year with a very elegant and merry table decoration. Silver animates sombre grey, delicate poppies in rosé brighten and refresh the scene.

Purpurne Tafelpracht
Table in magnificent purple

Adventstee-Einladung
Invitation to Advent tea

Weihnachts-Rendezvous
Christmas rendezvous

Sternstunde der TischArt
Star-studded table art

Happy New Year
Happy New Year

WinterRendezvous
WinterRendezvous

Eisblumen könnten symbolisch für die letzte und kälteste Jahreszeit stehen. Und dennoch kann diese nicht minder warmherzig, gefühlvoll und sinnlich bei Tischdekorationen interpretiert werden.
Wenn auch die Blüten nicht mehr allzu reichhaltig vorhanden sind, so stehen dann vielleicht mehr Naturmaterialien zusammen mit ihren Accessoires im Vordergrund. Dazu die Texturen, Strukturen und Materialeigenschaften ergeben ein reizvolles und dekoratives Bild, werden sie stimmig mit den typischen winterlichen Attributen komponiert.
Was der Sommer an strahlender Leuchtkraft, der Herbst an Form- und Farbvielfalt bereithält, ist beim Winter das Kerzenlicht.
Ihr Schein taucht die liebevoll gedeckten Tische in eine Stimmung, die ans Herz geht.
Purpurne Tafelpracht, warmes Rot ist ganzjährig in Mode. Speziell zur Winterzeit wird es in Kombination mit edlem Grau ein wenig gezähmt und untermalt dennoch die festliche Pracht.
Adventstee-Einladung, Farben und der Duft von Honigwachs, Zimt, Anis und Nelken verdichten sich zu einer stimmungsvollen Tischszenerie, die die Kälte des Winters vergessen lässt.
Weihnachts-Rendezvous, Erinnerungen an Weihnachten in frühen Kindertagen werden wach. Doch traditionelles Rot und Grün wird hier neu und zeitgemäß definiert.
Sternstunde der TischArt, Schwarz und Weiß, Farben, die die Konzentration auf das Wesentliche lenken. Eine Tischdekoration, die die Bedeutung des Weihnachtsfestes mit Ruhe und Klarheit trägt.
Happy New Year, Jahreswechsel mit edler und festlich wirkender Tafeldekoration. Silber belebt trübes Grau, zarter Mohn in Rosé hellt frisch und belebend auf.

Stühle (Lazis), Geschirr (Broste Design), Gläser (Veip), Gästebuch (Räder), Kerzen (AV), Gedeck (Becker), Monogramm (Cane Classic), Kisseneuphorbie (Pinaruh)

chairs (Lazis), dishes (Broste Design), glasses (Veip), guest book (Räder), candles (AV), place settings (Becker), silver letters (Cane Classic), dried vines (Pinaruh)

Table in magnificent purple
Purpurne Tafelpracht

The rich opulence of the Burgundy velvet sets the mood for this festive winter table. Outside, Mother Nature is dressed first in dull reds and browns, fading then to pale greys and white, and autumn showers of leaves have left behind bare branches on trees and bushes. But inside there is a glow of sensual magnificence. Behind tightly-closed doors the soft flowing lines of luxurious textiles and warm colours create a cosy atmosphere immune to winter cold. Even so, the guests also include barren vegetation from outside. Bundles of twigs, leafless vines and winter-faded fibres are entwined with carnation blossoms on long stems.

Star shapes and the glow of metal here and there make the first announcements of the approaching Christmas festivities. Even without the sheen of gold or silver, the stars with their pale violet tones underscore the excited anticipation of the festivities and the jolly atmosphere of dining at home.

Die schwere Opulenz des dunkelrotfarbenen Samtes bestimmt den festlich geprägten Wintertisch. Wo sich draußen die Natur erst in ein dumpfes Rotbraun, später in ein tristes, müdes Grauweiß gekleidet und der herbstliche Blätterregen kahle Bäume und Sträucher dagelassen hat, erstrahlt drinnen sinnliche Pracht. Hinter fest verschlossenen Türen schaffen weiche Textilien, üppig-fließende Stoffe und eine warme Farbigkeit anheimelnde Atmosphäre, die der winterlichen Kälte trotzt. Dennoch ist die kahle Vegetation zu Gast geladen. Zweigbündelungen, blattlose Ranken und winterfahle Fasern verbinden sich mit den Nelkenblüten auf langem Stängel. Erste Sternenattribute und Metalleffekte dazwischen künden vom bevorstehenden Weihnachtsfest. Auch ohne dass sie in gleißend glänzendem Gold oder Silber erstrahlen, unterstreichen sie in ihrem aufgehellten Violett erwartungsfrohe Festlichkeit und stimmungsvolle Tafelkultur daheim.

Purpurne Tafelpracht. Die kräftige, opulente Farbe des samtenen Tischbelages wird mit einer leichtfüßigen und geradezu hochbeinigen Floraldekoration kombiniert. Das dezente und schlicht wirkende Tafelgeschirr tut natürlich ein übriges, um die neue, sinnliche Leichtigkeit zu unterstreichen: Kelchähnliche Glasvasen und schlanke Spitzkerzen, die sich auf ihren Besenbeinchen nach oben recken. Oder auch die dünnen Weidenzweige, auf denen das winterliche Fasergeäst – von Kabelbindern gehalten – zu schweben scheint. Alles folgt der aufstrebenden und damit Leichtigkeit vermittelnden Richtung. Auserlesen sind die dünnen Zweige der Kisseneuphorbie, aus denen die besenförmigen Kerzenständer gearbeitet sind. Die Halterung aus Walzblei bildet zu dieser rauhen Natürlichkeit den gewollten wie schmückenden Kontrast. Das gilt auch für den Schmuck des Serviettentäschchens mit dem Monogramm eines jeden Gastes, das auf aufgeklebten Blütenblättern und Kiefernnadeln ruht. Das Gästebuch ziert ein mit Nelkenblütenblättern beklebter und überwachster Stern.

Table in magnificent purple. The rich opulent colour of the velvet tablecloth is combined with a light-footed floral decoration standing on tall stems. The tasteful and simple table setting assumes an additional function to underscore the new, sensual lightness: goblet-shaped glass vases and slim tapered candles stand tall on broom-like supports. Or the fine wicker twigs on which the wintry branchwork – secured with cords – appears to float and sway. In its quest to follow its upwards path, the arrangement gives the impression of weightlessness.

Specially selected are the thin, delicate pine twigs forming the broom-shaped candle holders. The rolled metal rings holding the "brooms" together provide the necessary contrast to this raw natural element. This also applies to the serviette decorations with their monogram for each guest resting on a bundle of glued flower petals and pine needles. The guest book is adorned with a waxed star of carnation petals.

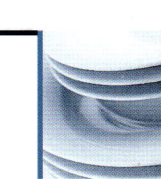

silk stars (Haymann), place settings (Becker), agave, dried vines (Pinaruh), hurricane lamps (Veip)

Seidensterne (Haymann), Gedeck (Becker), Agave, Kisseneuphorbie (Pinaruh), Windlichter (Veip)

Purpurne Tafelpracht. Nicht immer kann sich das Streben in die Höhe als sinnvoll oder praktikabel erweisen. Dennoch leidet die sinnliche Ausstrahlung nicht. Auch in einer Floraldekoration, die der Längsausrichtung des Tisches folgt, können die Farbigkeit, die Materialpracht und die Einbeziehung wintertrockener Naturmaterialien ihre gestalterische Vollendung erfahren. Die Rosenblüten, die kurz in heißes Wachs getaucht wurden, erhalten unterm Wachskorsett lange ihre Schönheit. Zu ihnen gesellen sich Früchte, Blätter, exotische Blüten und Schmuckelemente in der breiten Palette der dunklen Rottöne auf einem Agavenblatt drapiert. Hinzugelegt können sie jederzeit ausgetauscht werden und damit, ganz nach Belieben, der Dekoration eine andere Ausstrahlung verleihen. Die Basis aus Trockengeäst erhält durch Maschendraht ihre Stabilität. In dieser über Wochen haltbaren Gestaltung werden sich aufgrund der üppigen Vielseitigkeit sicherlich die Augen der hier Tafelnden entdeckend und suchend verlieren. Ein optischer Schmaus, an den sich jeder Gast lange erinnern wird!

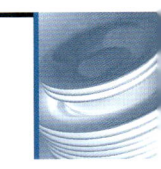

Table in magnificent purple. Arrangements that reach up towards the sky are not always sensible or practical. But that does not mean that the sensual ambience must be lost. A floral decoration laid across the table can also be a hit with all the same resplendent colours and materials, including the winter-dried natural materials The rose petals, which have been briefly immersed in hot wax, retain their youthful beauty longer inside their waxy corsets.
Their table companions include fruit, leaves, exotic flowers and decorative accessories from the entire red spectrum draped on an agave leaf. Simply placed in the arrangement, they can be changed around anytime to achieve a different ambience. The base of dried branchwork is given additional stability by mesh wire. This creation, which will keep for weeks, is sure to attract the admiring glances of every guest approaching the table – not least due to its interesting diversity. A sight for sore eyes that guests will remember for a long time!

Kissen (Lazis), Kerzen (AV), Gefäße (Edelman),
Geschirr (Becker), Fransengimpe (Halbach)
cushions (Lazis), candles (AV), vases (Edelman),
dishes (Becker), fringed gimp (Halbach)

Invitation to Advent tea

Adventstee-Einladung

Die Teezeremonie nach fernöstlichem Vorbild in einer schlichten, ruhigen und damit fast kontemplativ wirkenden Atmosphäre findet zunehmend Begeisterte. Nach den hektischen Stunden lassen der Duft würzigen Tees, Kerzenlicht und weiche Sitzkissen eine Oase entstehen, in der Ruhe und Besinnung Platz haben. Besonders in der Winterzeit ist die Sehnsucht vieler Menschen danach sehr groß. Warmwirkende Farben, stimmungsgebendes Kerzenlicht, aber auch Silber, Grün und Weiß verbinden sich zu einer Szenerie, die alle Sinne anspricht.

The tea ceremony borrowed from Oriental traditions in a simple, peaceful and therefore almost contemplative atmosphere is becoming increasingly popular. After the hectic hours of a long stressful day, the spicy aroma of tea, soft candlelight and soft cushions become an oasis of peace and meditation. Especially in the winter season many people yearn for such a respite. Warm and cosy colours, glowing candlelight and silver, green and white combine to make a settting that invites all the senses!

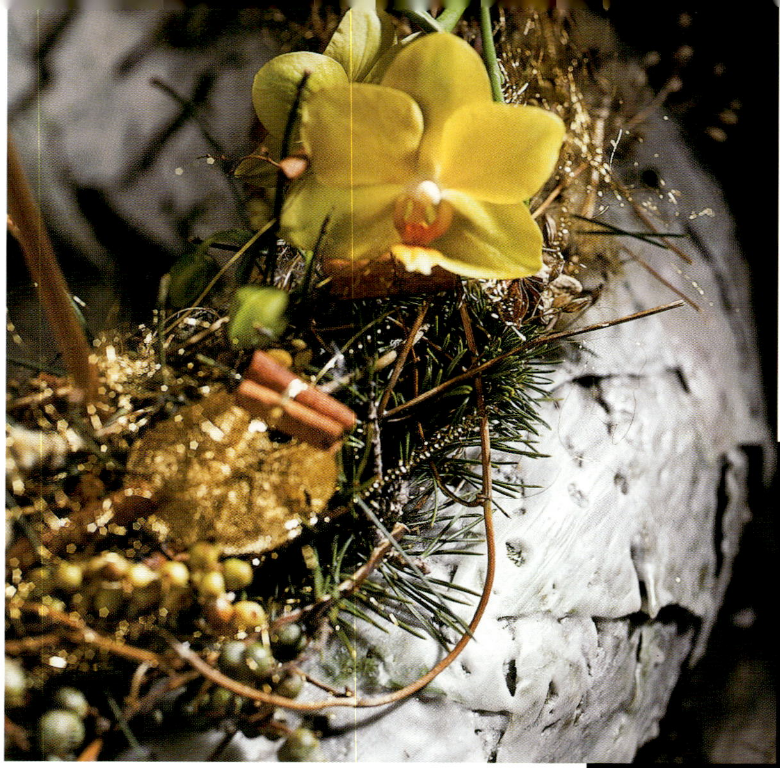

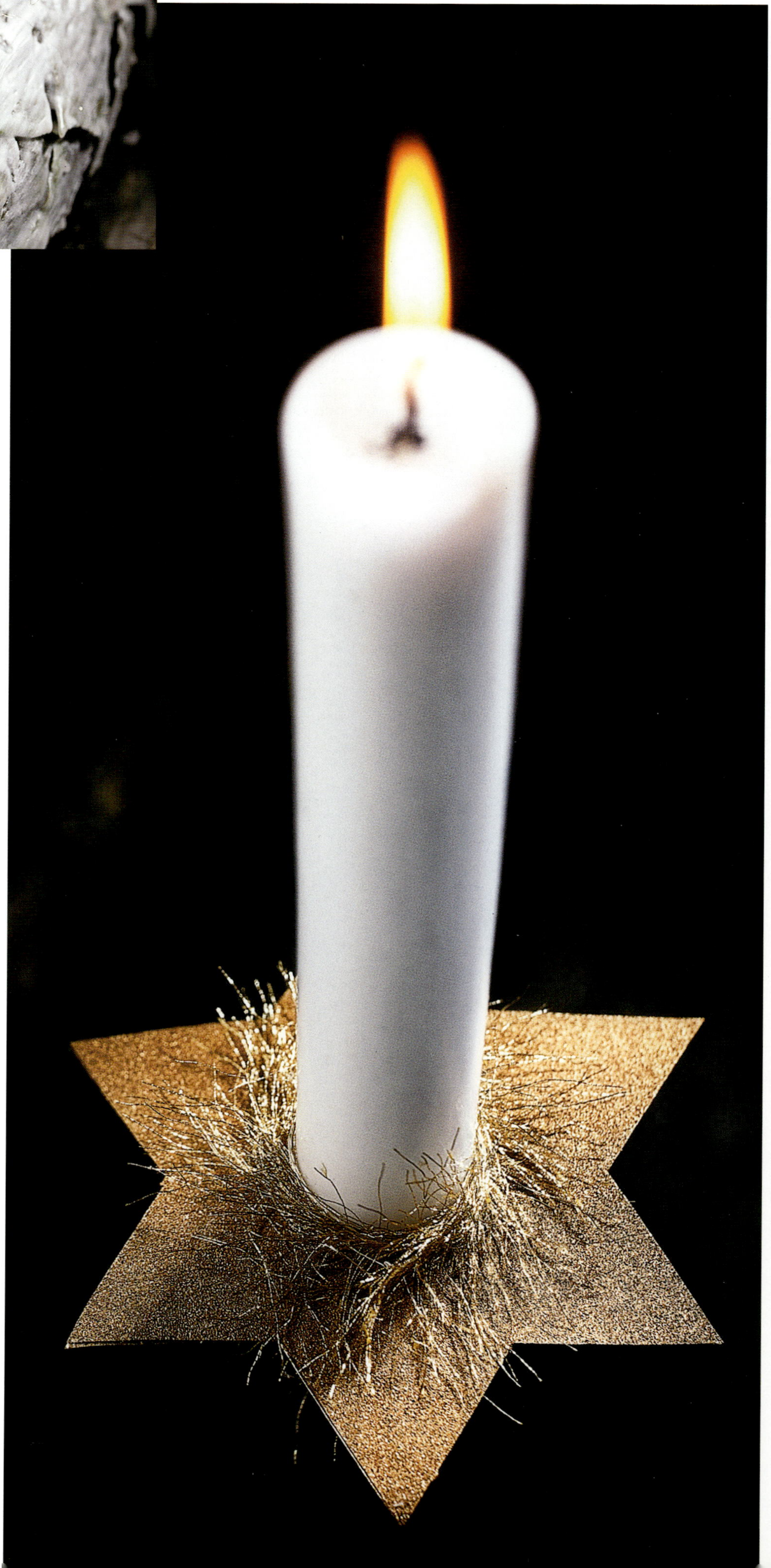

Adventstee-Einladung. Zimtstangen und mit Nelken gespickte Orangen im Kerzenlicht, Kandisstäbchen zum Süßen des heißen Tees als Platzanweiser.
Kostbar wirkende Orchideenblüten in kleinen Wasserröhrchen bilden den einzigen farbigen Frischakzent auf dem wachsüberzogenen Efeublattkranz. Er dient gleichzeitig als Basis der vielen erhöht platzierten Kerzen. Praktisch wie zierend sind die schlichten, sternförmigen Untersetzer, da sie zusammen mit dem Fransenband auch als Tropfschutz für die Stabkerzen dienen. In ihrer fernöstlichen Schlichtheit entsprechen diese liebevoll aufeinander abgestimmten Details gleichzeitig dem Bedürfnis nach sinnlich-festlich wirkenden Attributen in der kalten Winterzeit.

Invitation to Advent tea. Cinnamon sticks and oranges spiked with cloves in the glow of candlelight. Rock candy on little stir-sticks to sweeten the hot tea and also double as name card holders. Costly-looking orchid blooms in miniature glass tubes provide the only note of freshness on the waxed ivy wreath, which also serves as the base for the tapered candles in their tall holders. These are both practical and decorative with their star-shaped supports which, together with the golden fringes, also catch the dripping wax from the candles. In their Oriental simplicity these so lovingly co-ordinated details satisfy the need for sensual-festive accents in the cold winter season.

Adventstee-Einladung. Der große Stern mit Maschendrahtkorsett und aus Trockenblättern gebildet, ist auch in waagerechter Position gleichermaßen zierender Mittelpunkt der Teezeremonie. Statt aufgesteckter Kerzen finden sich hier Honigwachsplatten als Sternschmuck, die zusammen mit den Zimtstangen und den mit den Nelken gespickten Orangen in der Wärme des Raumes ihren weihnachtlichen Duft entfalten.
Zu Schmuckelementen geklebt liegen sie auch vor jedem Gast auf den Servietten und aufgerollten Platzsets. Die mit Blattgold überzogene Platte ist einerseits Präsentationsgrundlage für den Stern, andererseits dient sie als Tischplatte, auf der auch die Teeschalen der Drumherumsitzenden abgestellt werden können.

Invitation to Advent tea. The oversized star, made of dried leaves with a corset of mesh wire, can likewise be the decorative focus of the tea ceremony in a horizontal position. Instead of candles this time, flat strips of beeswax give the finishing touch to the star-shaped wreath.
Together with the cinnamon sticks and orange stars spiked with cloves, the decorative serviette rings for the guests fill the warm cosy room with a heavenly Christmas scent.
And the gold-plated platform is not just a presentation platter for the star, it also serves as a table on which the guests can set down their teacups.

Holzgefäße (Pizarro), Kissen (Lazis), Kerzen (Arte), Bienenwachs (Imker)

wooden pots (Pizarro), cushions (Lazis), candles (Arte), beeswax (Imker)

Stühle (Lazis), Kerzen (AV), Gedeck (Becker)

chairs (Lazis), candles (AV), dishes (Becker)

Christmas rendezvous
Weihnachts-Rendezvous

A classic decoration with typical Christmas colours and shapes. The traditional red-green for Advent and Christmas is not at all too heavy or compact here. On the contrary, the dark red and Burgundy, combined with the warm yellows and fresh shades of orange, provide a merry component for traditional festivities. Naturally the upward-reaching slim forms also play a decisive role in creating the light-hearted ambience of this table decoration.

Fruit from the year`s harvest, gathered on autumn walks through fields and forests, ties in with the wintry attributes – such as dried branches, candles and aromatic spices – which are already announcing the Christmas celebration.

Eine in Farbe und Formenausprägung klassische Festdekoration mit starkem Zeitbezug.

Das traditionelle Rot-Grün zu Advent und Weihnachten wirkt hier keinesfalls schwer oder kompakt. Vielmehr bringen das tiefe Rot und Bordeaux im Zusammenspiel mit warmen gelblichen und frisch-fröhlich wirkenden orangen Tönen eine heitere Komponente tradierter Festlichkeit. Natürlich spielen auch die überschlanken und hoch aufstrebenden Formen eine entscheidende Rolle für die Leichtigkeit ausstrahlende Tischgestaltung.

Die Früchte des Jahres, im späten Herbst bei Wanderungen durch Wald und Feld gesammelt, verbinden sich mit winterlichen Attributen, wie Trockenzweigen, Kerzen und duftenden Gewürzen, die bereits vom Weihnachtsfest künden.

Weihnachts-Rendezvous. Ein mittiger Stab gibt den Fruchtkegeln die Haltung. Um ihn sind die beerenbesetzten Zweige, sich unten verdichtend und verdickend, zur Spitze hin stark verjüngend, mit Draht gewickelt.

Als Fuß dienen mit Zimtstangen beklebt Holzklötze, als Top Zimtsterne, die die Stumpenkerze tragen. Übrigens: Werden die Fruchtkegel nicht längerfristig als Tischdekoration benötigt, geben sie auch in anderer Zusammenstellung auf Sideboards oder Regalen einen festlichen Schmuck ab. Damit auch im Blickfeld der an dieser Tafel Sitzenden Kerzenlicht erstrahlt, finden sich einige Stumpenkerzen auf Zimt beklebten und Beerengeschmückten Holzquadern. Auch die Tischplatte ist komplett mit Zimt bestreut. Die Servietten erhalten als Schmuckakzent eine „Zapfenspindel", die kunstvoll aus einem mit Golddraht und „Angelhair" umwickelten Holzstab, vergoldetem Blatt und dem Kiefernzapfen besteht.

Christmas rendezvous. A central pole gives the necessary support for the berry-laden vines and branches, which, fixed with wires, taper upwards like sharply elongated cones.

The base is made of wooden blocks decorated with rows of cinnamon sticks. The crowning glory: the cinnamon stars, each holding a thick candle aloft. By the way, if the fruit cones are no longer required to decorate the table, they can be used in other interesting variations to make festive arrangements on a sideboard or shelves.

To supplement the "heavenly" candlelight for the table guests down below, on the table are thick candles on matching cinnamon-adorned blocks with thick collars of red berries.

As a finishing touch, the entire tabletop is strewn with cinnamon sticks. The serviettes also receive their own decorative accessories in the form of pine cone sceptres, which are cones on slender wooden sticks artistically wound about with gold wires and angel hair, resting on a gold-plated leaf.

129

Tabletts, Teegläser (Des Pots), Metallschale (Inter Globe), Sterne (Florissima), Zapfen (Pinaruh), Lampen (Hillo), Kerzen (Arte)

trays, tea glasses (Des Pots), stars (Florissima), metal dish (Inter Globe), pine cones (Pinaruh), lamps (Hillo), candles (Arte)

Weihnachts-Rendezvous. Eine Alternative zur klassisch aufstrebenden Gestaltung ist die Girlande. Schon im alten Rom wurden Fruchtzweige in einander verwunden, um damit Türbögen, Fensternischen oder auch lange Festtafeln zu schmücken. Die traditionelle, auf Rot basierende Farbigkeit macht im Zusammenspiel mit natürlichen Tönen die moderne Interpretation aus.

Die Girlande verbindet die Kerzenaufstellung auf den quadratischen Tabletts. Bestandteil der Gestaltung sind auch die Kiefernzapfen, die die mit Golddraht befestigten Namensschildchen der Gäste tragen.

Christmas rendezvous. An alternative to classic upright creations is the garland. Even back in ancient Rome, fruit branches were intertwined to decorate doorways, windowsills and long dinner tables. Traditionally based on red, natural tones are added here for a more modern interpretation. The garland links the symmetrically-placed candles on the rectangular table. Another basic component of this table decoration: the pine cones which bear the name tags of the guests affixed on gold wires.

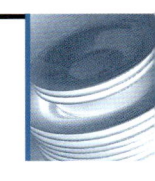

Die Farbe Schwarz. Was wäre ihre weihnachtliche Festlichkeit, wenn sie nicht durch die Konträrfarbe Weiß und edlen Silberglanz ihre besondere Untermalung erhielte. Kaum eine andere Farbkombination strahlt eindeutiger und besser winterliche Eleganz und festliche Klarheit aus. Meist unterstützt Reduzierung oder Konzentration auf Weniges ein schlichtes Ambiente. So auch hier. Denn der Stern steht als gestalterisches Element und als das typisches Festsymbol ganz im Mittelpunkt. Gleichgültig ob als Blütenstern, wie bei der edelsten und kostbarsten aller Winterblüherin, der Christrose, oder bei den strahlend klar widerleuchtenden Stern-Accessoires auf dem langen und bewegt schwingenden Stab: Diese überhöhte Theatralik der Tischinszenierung symbolisiert das winterliche Sternenfunkeln in höchster Vollendung!

The colour black. But without the contrasting white and elegant silver highlights in the decoration, its feeling of Christmas festivities would be lost. Hardly any other colour combination can better express such wintry elegance and festive clarity. Usually it is the purposeful restriction of colours and a focus on minimalism that create this simple look. And here. As a creative element and also a typical symbol for Christmas, the star is made the "star of the show" here. Whether in the star-shaped Christmas rose – the most elegant and costly of all winter flowers – or in the clear lines of the brilliant star accessories on their long, swaying poles: the over-the-top theatrical effects of this table decoration play the role of wintry skies to absolute perfection!

Star-studded table art
Sternstunde der TischArt

Stühle (Lazis), Geschirr (Becker), Gipssockel (Blümchen & Ko), Glasschale, Glassockel (Veip), Christbaumkugeln (Inge-Glas), Servietten (ASA)

chairs (Lazis), dishes (Becker), plaster pedestals (Blümchen & Ko), glass dish, glass base (Veip), Christmas tree decorations (Inge-Glas), serviettes (ASA)

Star-studded table art. Making virtue of necessity can sometimes be a simple and equally clever idea. Who does not feel sad when treasured Christmas-tree decorations get broken. It would really be a shame to carelessly throw them away. Simply turned upside-down, filled with water and placed side-by-side in a glass dish, these handmade glass treasures serve as vases for the delicate star-shaped flowers. The star symbol is also found in the serviette holder. It is artistically formed of silver wire and angel hair, a tangled mass of thin metal wires. A fresh note is added by the Christmas rose, its stem covered with silver plate, both to prevent it from drying out and to add a final decorative touch. Christmas roses also adorn the mounds of privet berries, which are given an additional wintry touch by the light dusting of sugar crystals. The stars hovering up above the scene are delicate and sweet-scented, wrapped around with natural fibres and fragrant carnation petals, all in white.

Overall, a table decoration which combines festive symbolism with a touch of elegance to make an artistic creation worthy of any table.

Sternstunde der TischArt. Aus der Not eine Tugend gemacht kann manchesmal die simple und gleichermaßen geniale Idee sein. Wer ärgert sich nicht, wenn beim Aufhängen kostbarer Christbaumkugeln aus Glas diese abbrechen. Zu schade wäre es, sie achtlos wegzuwerfen.

Einfach umgedreht, mit Wasser gefüllt und auf einer Glasschale zusammengestellt können die mundgeblasenen Kostbarkeiten den zarten Blütensternen als Vase dienen. Das Sternsymbol findet sich auch beim Serviettenschmuck.

Es ist aus Silberdraht und „Angelhair" geformt, einem an Engelhaar erinnernden Gewusel aus zarten Metallfäden. Als Frischblumenakzent eine Christrose, deren Stängelende gegen zu schnelles Austrocknen und gleichermaßen als zusätzliche Zierde mit Blattsilber bedeckt ist. Christrosen zieren auch aus Ligusterbeeren gearbeitete Formen, denen das Bestreuen mit Zuckerkristallen ein Hauch Winterlichkeit verleiht. Die über allem schwebenden Sterne sind zart und duftig, mit weißen Naturfasern und weißen, duftenden Nelkenblütenblättern umwickelt. Im Ganzen eine Tischdekoration, bei der sich eine festliche Symbolik und ein Hauch von Eleganz zur Tafelgestaltung vereinen.

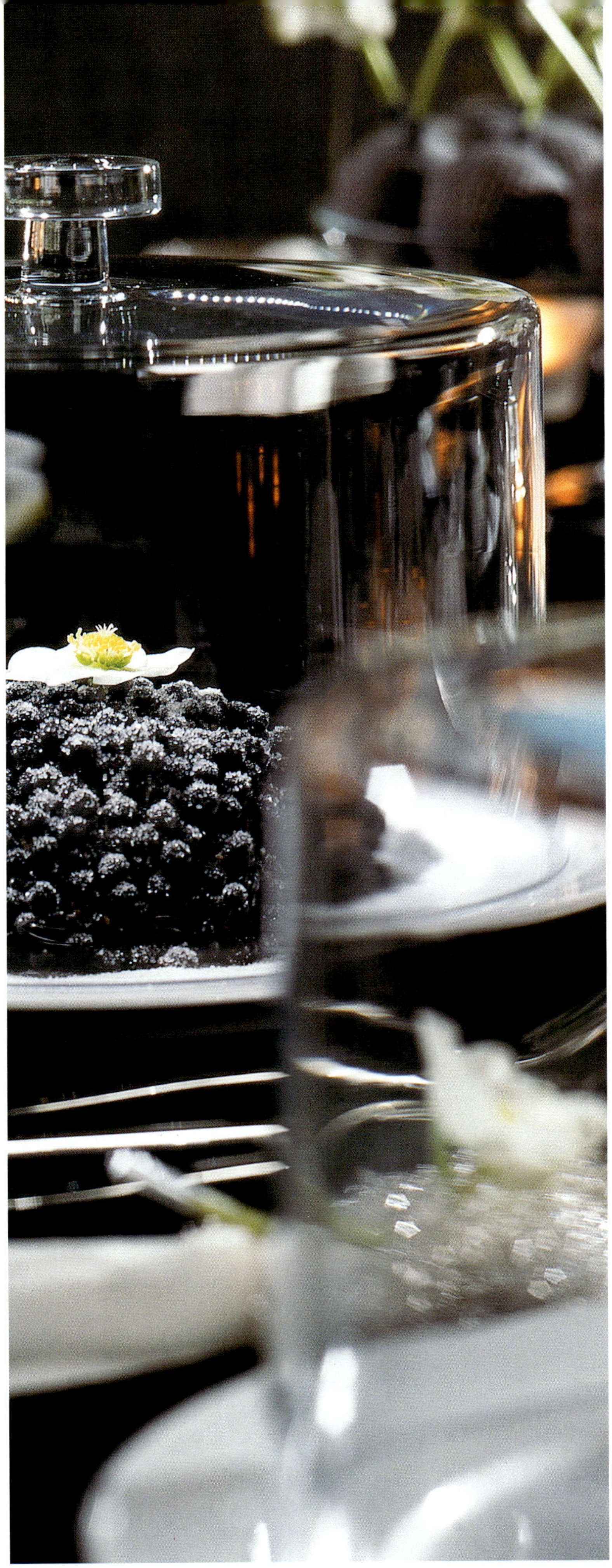

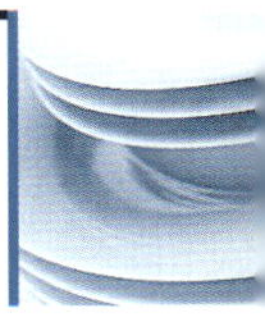

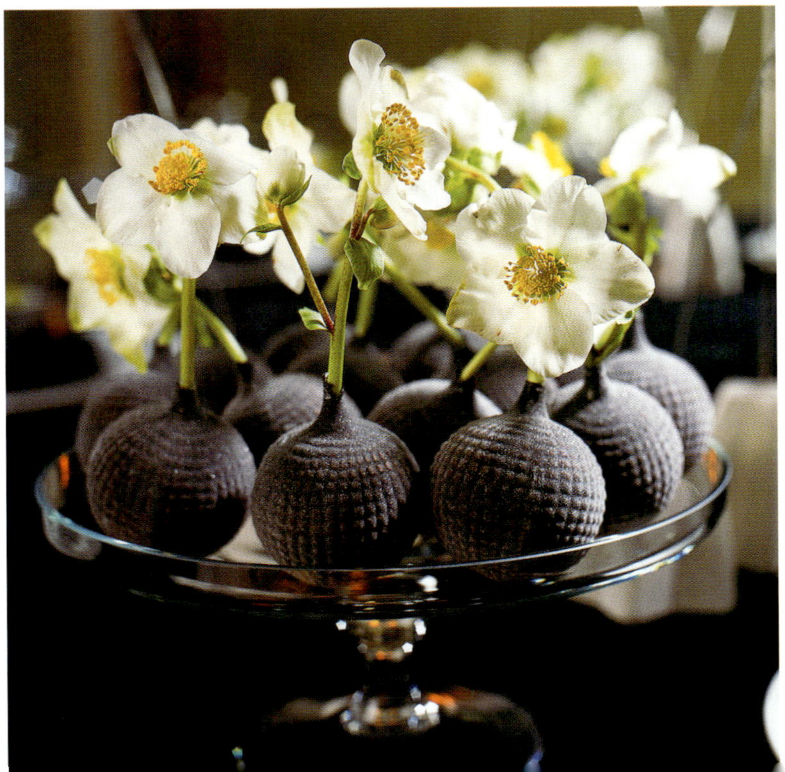

136

Sternstunde der TischArt.
Wem der harte Schwarz-Weiß-Kontrast zu stark wirkt und die festliche Symbolik nicht nur auf die Sternform reduziert bleiben soll, der mag sich sicher für eine farblich mildere Variante erwärmen. Kaltes, klares Weiß wird zu einem matten Silber oder aufgehelltem Anthrazit.
Deshalb sind Gefäße für den Blütenschmuck aus weißer Orchideenblüte, Silberkugel und Ligusterbeeren mit der Baumflechte aus den heimischen Wälder strukturgebend beklebt.
Schwarz ist durch eine Vielzahl gläserner Accessoires und Geschirr-Bestandteile in seiner dominanten Wirkung geschmälert. Mattes und glänzendes Silber verbindet zum weiß. Höchste Festlichkeit erstrahlt auf hohem Metallständer in Form von Teelichtern hinter Drahtgewebe. Das weiche Formenspiel der großen und kleinen mattsilbernen Kugeln, die wie zufällig über die Länge der Tafel verteilt sind, harmoniert mit edlen Kristallgläsern und feinstem Porzellan. Ein Ensemble, das höchste Tischkultur ausstrahlt, eine Tafel, für festliche Gastlichkeit in der langen Nacht am Heiligen Abend.

Star-studded table art. Those who find the strict black-and-white contrast too much and who do not wish to reduce festive symbolism to just stars will perhaps warm up to an alternative with a milder colour scheme. Cold clear white is toned down to matte silver or pale anthracite. Therefore, the vases holding the floral arrangements — white orchids, silver balls and privet berries — are covered with a natural-looking layer of bark from local forests.
The dominant effect of the colour black is reduced by adding a number of glass accessories and dishes. A festive mood is created by the tall metal stands holding aloft tiny candles inside mesh wire boxes. The soft interplay of shapes between the matte silver balls in different sizes, strewn apparently at random over the surface of the table, harmonizes with the noble crystal goblets and finest China dishes. An ensemble which exudes an aura of fine dining, and a table fit for festive hospitality in the long night before Christmas.

Leuchter (Drescher), Kerzen (AV), Christbaumkugel (Inge-Glas), Gläser (Krömer Zolnir), Teller `Berlin` von KPM (Becker), Stühle (Lazis)

candleholders (Drescher), candles (AV), Christmas tree decorations (Inge-Glas), glasses (Krömer Zolnir), `Berlin` plates from KPM (Becker), chairs (Lazis)

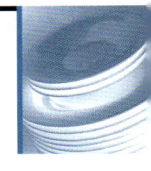

Spiegel (Boss elitaire), **Stühle** (Lazis), **Leuchter, Etagere** (Boss elitaire), **Christbaumkugeln** (Inge-Glas), **Serviettenringe** (Lebert), **Gästebuch** (Räder), **Gläser, Sektkühler** (Becker)

mirror (Boss elitaire), chairs (Lazis), candleholder, tiered serving dish (Boss elitaire), Christmas tree decorations (Inge-Glas), serviette rings (Lebert), guest book (Räder), glasses, champagne cooler (Becker)

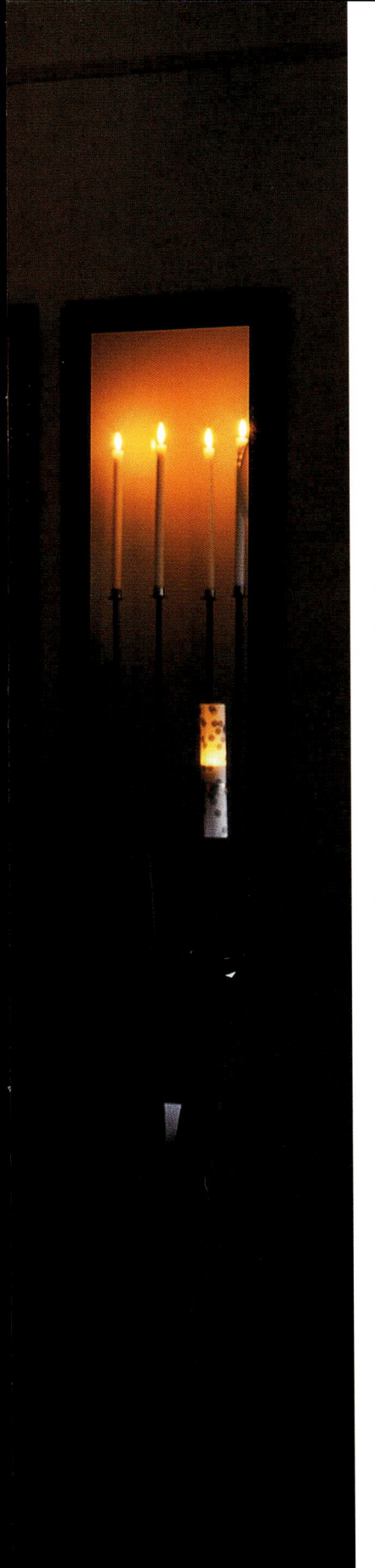

Happy New Year

Happy New Year

Der Silvesterabend. Krönender Abschluss des Jahres, in dem sich die Kunst erlesener Tafelkultur ein letztes Mal und im wahrsten Sinne des Wortes zu geselliger Höchstform aufschwingt. Denn hier schwebt, an Luftballons gehalten, der Schmuck über der Tischfläche. Alles wirkt leicht und unbeschwert, wie in den schlanken Sektflöten der perlende Sekt, das typische Getränk für den Jahreswechsel. Und selbst die bewusst gewählten, zarten Pastellfarben unterstreichen den fröhlichen, beschwingten Übergang vom Ende der alten zu einer neuen Zeitrechnung. „Happy New Year" wünschen die mit Helium gefüllten und damit unter der Decke schwebenden Ballons mit ihrer blumigen Fracht. Eine Reminiszenz an das Vergangene mit dem erwartungsfrohen Blick auf die neue Jahres-Zeit!

New Year`s Eve. The grand finale of the year for elevating the art of fine dining one last time, and in every sense of the word, to the highest social form.
Because here the table decorations float over the surface of the table, suspended from silver balloons. Everything appears as carefree and light as the bubbles in the champagne – the typical wine for toasting in the new year. Even the carefully-chosen delicate pastels underscore the merry, light-hearted passage from the old year to the new.
"Happy New Year" shout the helium-filled balloons, as they float and sway beneath the ceiling carrying their fragrant passengers. A fond look back mixed with hopeful anticipation for what the future will bring!

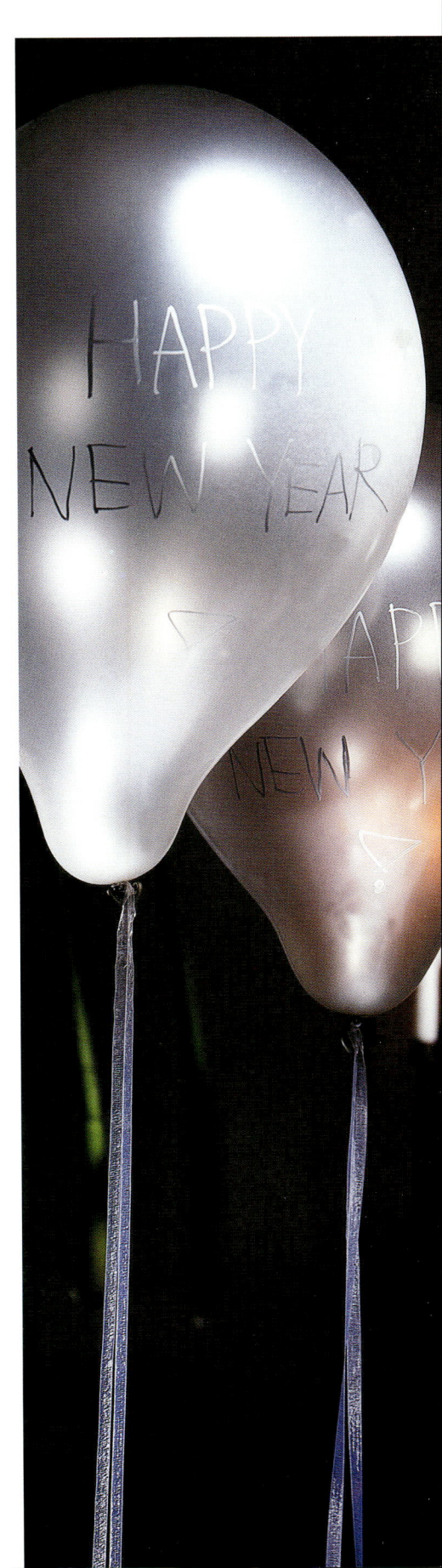

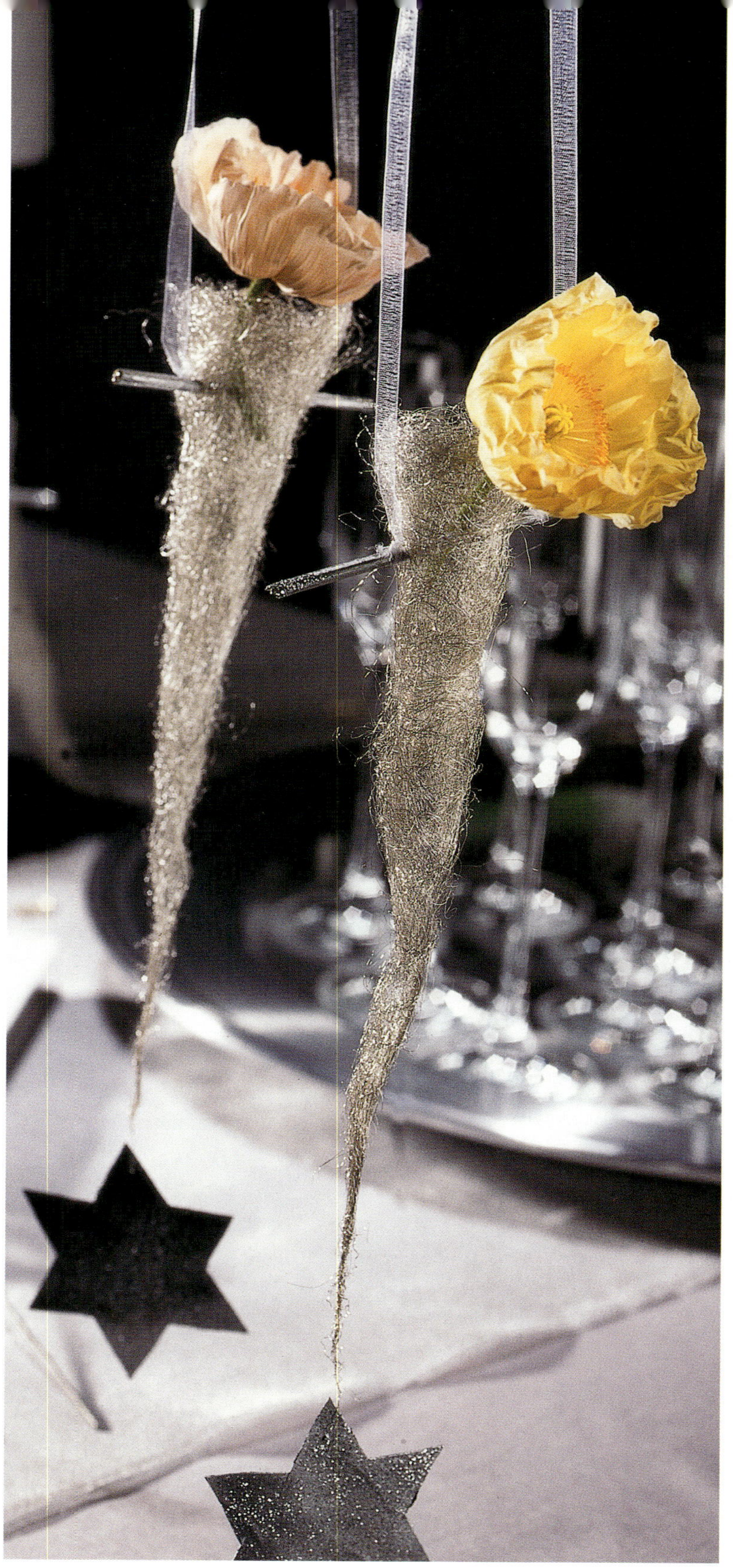

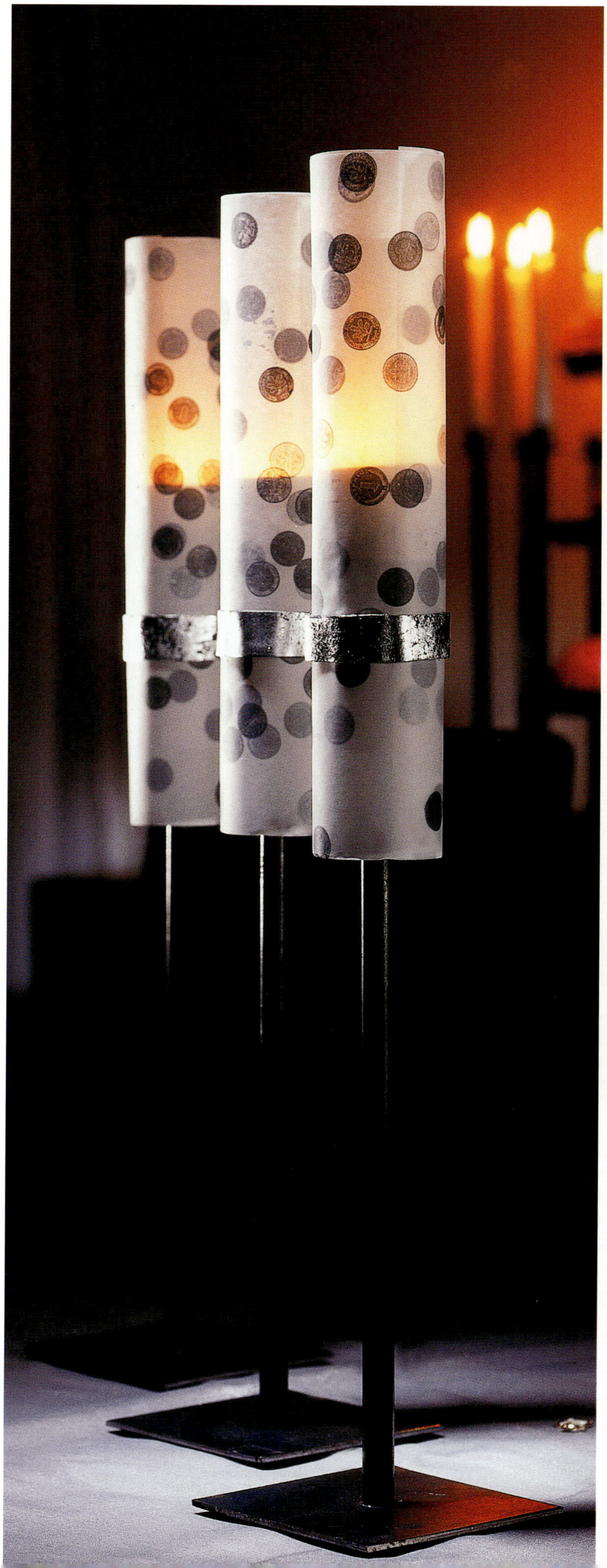

Happy New Year. Mohnblüten, Synonym für Leichtigkeit, Zartheit und jahresübergreifende Verbindung zieren nicht nur die Servietten der Gäste, sondern sind auch die blumige Fracht der Ballons. Ihr silbernes Körbchen ist aus „Angelhair" gestaltet, das um Glasröhrchen gewickelt wird.

Für die Ballonseilschaft werden zarte Textilbänder an quer durch die Tüte gesteckten Stäben befestigt. Sterne dienen als notwendiger Ballast, um die duftigen Passagiere auf der gewünschten Höhe zu halten. Das Luftballonsymbol findet sich auch bei den Platzkarten in Form von Stickern. Die Namen der Gäste werden mit wasserfestem Silberstift auf ein entsprechend geschnittene Stück Folie geschrieben. Der Kupferpfennig, der fürs anbrechende Jahr Glück und Erfolg wünschen soll, ist mehrmals auf Pergaminpapier kopiert und dieses widerum in eine Laminierrolle eingeschweißt. So werden sie um Kerzen oder auch Lampen gestellt und geben stimmungsvolle Lichtatmosphäre. Glückverheißende Symbolik für die letzte Nacht des Jahres.

Happy New Year. Poppies, the epitome of light and delicate elements and a link between the years, adorn not only the serviettes of the guests, but are also the floral freight of the balloons.
Their silvery baskets are made of angel air wound around glass tubes. Connecting the baskets to the balloons are delicate textile ribbons which are tied to small pins stuck through the baskets. Stars attached to the tips of the cone-shaped baskets serve as the necessary ballast to keep the fragant passengers at the desired height. The balloon symbol is found again in the place cards in the form of stickers. The names of the guests are written in waterproof silver marker on pieces of transparent foil cut in the shape of balloons. A copper penny – believed to bring good luck in the coming year – is copied all over a sheet of parchment paper, which is then laminated and rolled together. These rolls can be used as shades for candles or lamps to create an idyllic glow of light. Good luck charms for the final night of the year.

Vase, Becher (Hillo), Fransenband (Senn),
Gimpe (Halbach), Teller (Leupold)

vase, silver cups (Hillo), fringed trim (Senn),
gimp (Halbach), plates (Leupold)

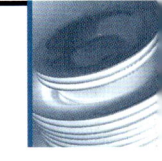

Happy New Year. Silberne Transparenz kann gleichermaßen leicht und unbeschwert den Jahresausklang festlich unterstreichen. Silberfarbene Ständervasen und Proteenblüten in frischem Rosé schmücken den Tisch für das Silvestermenü. Die Vasen sind zusätzlich mit Fransenband und Laminierfolie – beschrieben mit Neujahrswünschen – versehen. Was rosig-pastellig nahezu schwebt, findet ein tischnahes Pendant in Form der Proteenblüten im silbernen Becher. Ein Pelz aus flusigem Samengespinst wird zur ungewöhnlichen Zier.
Und last but not least haben auch die blattversilberten Äpfel Platz auf der Festtafel, ein weiteres Symbol, das dem Beschenkten Glück und Erfolg im neuen Jahr wünscht.

Happy New Year. Silver transparency can highlight the end of the year in a festive way that is both light and carefree. Silvery vases in metal stands and *Protea* flowers in refreshing rosé adorn the dinner table on New Year`s Eve. The vases are additionally decorated with feathery fringes at the base and a clear sheet of plastic, rolled and inscribed with New Year`s wishes. Complementing the rosy pastels on high are *Protea* flowers in silver cups down below on the table. The fluffy cloud of plumed seeds provides an unusual and decorative finishing touch. And last but not least, the silver-plated apples find their rightful place on the festive table, yet another symbol of good luck for the guests in the new year.

Thank you
Danke

Allen, die an diesem Buch mitgewirkt haben, sei an dieser Stelle herzlich gedankt:

Frank Pieper
　　für die gesamte Konzeption, die Ideen, die Durchführung
Beatrix Renzel, Astrid Herrmann-Rieper, Heiko Bleuel, Othilie Glack, Jasmin Centner, Akie Ishida, Nicole Mauche und Britta Kroggel
　　für die floristischen Ausführungen
Harry Gregg
　　für die technischen Aufbauten
Patrick Pantze, Stephan Röcken und Jörg Manegold
　　für die Fotoarbeiten
Silvia Bodewig und Heike Beck
　　für die grafische Realisation
Silvia Weichert
　　für die gesamte grafische Betreuung
Hella Henckel-Bruckhaus
　　für den Text
Janet Brümmer
　　für die Übersetzung ins Englische
dem gesamten ‚profil floral'-Team
　　für die Begleitung

vielen, die uns ihre Räume zum Fotografieren überlassen haben und folgenden Firmen für die Überlassung von Produkten für die Fotoproduktion:

Becker/Minden (Geschirr und Bestecke), ABA/Niestetal, Arte/Mainhardt, ASA/Höhr-Grenzhausen, AV/Abstatt, Blümchen & Ko/Ibbenbühren, Boss Elitaire/Albstadt, Braucke/Hemer, Broste Design/DK-Lynby, Cane Classic/Kempten, Des Pots/Münster, Drescher/Schwebheim, Edelman/Ransbach-Baumbach, Florholz/Hamburg, Florissima/Hamburg, Haans/NL-Tilburg, Hakbijl/NL-Lelystad, Halbach/Remscheid-Lüttringhausen, Haymann/Norken, Henry Dean/B-Massenhoven, Hillo/DK-Slagelse, Ikea, Inge-Glas/Neustadt-Cbg., Inter Globe/NL-Enschede, Kayak/Kalkar, Kehrle/Weißenhorn, Krömer-Zolnir/Nienstädt, Lazis/Bingen, Leupold/Schauenstein, Lebert/Berlin, Moulin Galland-Mavet/Maintal, Pinaruh/Lünen, Pulsar/Dreieich, Räder/Bochum, Ronkenstein/Hilden, Pizarro/NL-Almere, Sandra Rich/Ransbach-Baumbach, Senn/CH-Basel, Steingaesser/Miltenberg, TEL/NL-Ootmarsum, Vaban/NL-Sittard, Veip/NL-Aalsmeer.

Floristik Marketing Service, GmbH, Ratingen/Minden, Januar 2000.

To everyone who took part in making this book, we would like to extend our heartfelt thanks, especially to:

Frank Pieper
　　for the overall conception, ideas and implementation
Beatrix Renzel, Astrid Herrmann-Rieper, Heiko Bleuel, Othilie Glack, Jasmin Centner, Akie Ishida, Nicole Mauche and Britta Kroggel
　　for the floristic arrangements
Harry Gregg
　　for the technology management
Patrick Pantze, Stephan Röcken and Jörg Manegold
　　for the photography
Silvia Bodewig and Heike Beck
　　for the graphics
Silvia Weichert
　　for the overall graphics management
Hella Henckel-Bruckhaus
　　for the texts
Janet Brümmer
　　for the translations into English
the entire ‚profil floral' team
　　for their support

many others who provided perfect locations for our photo shoots and the following companies for providing their products for the photos: